PROPHETIC POTPOURRI

H.B.* & His/Her Bible Adventures

Volume 6   by H.B. George Harper

* Human Being

Library of Congress Catalog Card Number: 86-81422
ISBN 0-934318-91-3

Published by H.B. Publications,
38 Cloverview, Helena, Montana 59601

Publishing Consultant:
Falcon Press Publishing Co., Inc.,
Helena and Billings, Montana

CONTENTS

A Brief Look at Bible History

2,000 B.C.   Abraham and Sarah were born just about exactly as many years before Jesus as you were born after Jesus.

After a few tales and observations about God's creation of the earth and the human beings on it, the *Bible* story of the Hebrew people's walk with God begins with the family journey out of Chaldea shortly after 2,000 B.C.

1,750 B.C.   Quickly the tales of their children unfold, but actually this little band of ancestors of the Hebrews grazed their sheep across Canaan for over two hundred years before Jacob's family ended up in Egypt with the sponsorship of Joseph who had made it big in the government there.

1,300 B.C.   For another four to five hundred years **1,250 B.C.**   they were to live there with no record of their life until the days of Moses. Then they followed God's leading to the Promised Land, and by 1,250 they sacked Jericho and entered the territory that would later be Israel.

1,000 B.C.   As 12 tribes led by "judges" or chiefs, they muscled their way into a land already occupied by people who didn't really want to give it up. It was 250 years before Saul began to form a "kingdom" out of the loose confederation of tribes. David got the job done, and for 40 years expanded the territorial boundaries of Israel to include a good chunk of the middle east. For another 40 years his son Solomon kept the new nation together, accomplishing what many *Bible* writers considered the central feat of Israel's history. He had the temple built in Jerusalem.

922 B.C.   But when Solomon died in 922 B.C., the nation split into two parts. Israel was the name kept by the northern kingdom; Judah was the southern portion and included Jerusalem with its temple.

722 B.C.   Exactly 200 years later, Israel was gone, wiped out by the Assyrians. Nineteen kings had come and gone, their stories preserved in the books of *Kings* and *Chronicles*. For the whole of those two centuries, there was constant fueding between the people who were trying to be faithful to the God of Moses and the Hebrews who had taken up worship of the gods and goddesses of the other nations. Sometimes one party would be in power, sometimes the other. And when the fires burned low on Yahweh's altars, there were prophets like Elijah and Elisha to stir the embers and throw on more fuel.

The history of the southern kingdom, Judah, paralleled that of Israel, with the same issues and struggles. Then, with God's help as Assyria's attention was diverted elsewhere, Judah survived for another 135 years. Kings lived longer, on the average, in Judah, because they had only 20 rulers (one queen included) in their 335-year history.

During this period of time when Israel was falling apart and Judah was holding on by the fingernails, the great prophets who shaped Hebrew and later Christian thought were preaching and writing.

587 B.C. Finally destroyed by the Babylonians in 587 B.C., the temple was gone and Jerusalem was in ruins. But a prophet named Huldah O.K.'d a manuscript that became the focal point for gathering the Torah, and urged King Josiah to renew the old celebration of the Passover. So when the people of Judah were also dispersed in captivity, they could keep their identity without a nation or temple.

538 B.C. Fifty years later the first band of Jews were allowed to return to Jerusalem. With noble intentions they began a temple-rebuilding project, then faltered for seventeen years. But in 520 B.C. they picked it up and finished the new temple four years later.

458 B.C. Not all the Jews hurried back to Judah. It was 80 years after the first group returned that Ezra led another "return." A decade later Nehemiah came to be the Persian-appointed governor. Most of the Jews in Babylon and Persia stayed in their new homelands and became leading citizens, developing Jewish scholarship that shaped up Hebrew scriptures and commentaries which still guide Judaism today.

167 B.C. However, the *Bible* story still centered on Judah, though we find few details of what happened there after the time of Nehemiah. We know that Alexander the Great took that part of the world away from Persian rule, and that after his death his divided empire still dominated Judah. By 167 B.C. one of those rulers, working out of Syria as his base, desecrated the altar of the Jerusalem temple by forcing sacrifices, even of pigs, to the Greek god Zeus. This act of Antiochus IV Epiphanes triggered a Jewish revolt led by the Maccabees. Three years later they restored the temple worship and set up Judah as an independent nation again.

63 B.C. That freedom lasted for a hundred years, but when Pompey and his legions established Rome's rule in 63 B.C. the Jews were never again to have an independent "homeland" until 1948 A.D.

By the time the Maccabean revolution was over, the period of writing the books found in the Hebrew *Bible* was ended. Later writings were added by some Jews dispersed in other nations, and accepted as part of the "Old Testament" by some Christian churches. Usually they are published together in a set of writings called "The Apocrypha."

1986 A.D. The books included in this last volume of our H.B. series on the Old Testament and following give us another look at what fourteen prophets of Israel and Judah put forth as the "word of the Lord" in their day. The sermons of Amos, the first prophet to write as well as preach his message, are here. Also here is the strange book of *Daniel*, probably the last of the writings, not counting the Apocryphal books.

I have tried to make the dull sections less dull, and the fascinating pictures and stories even more vivid. Now you use your imagination and judgment. Obviously these prophets don't all agree with each other on every point. You can have your opinion too. But first ask yourself, "What would they be saying to us in our world today?"

EZEKIEL

Weird Scenes and Common Sense

All of Jeremiah's message did not fall on deaf ears. The two ears of a young man named Ezekiel, priestly son of Buzi, heard them, and the heart and mind of the young priest gave them a home. And, though he is not mentioned in *Jeremiah*, Ezekiel joined the older prophet in pronouncing the message of doom to an unrepentant Judah. Most of his harsh words were launched during that last frustrating period of Judah's history between the first exile of Jehoiachin and other Jewish leaders and the final destruction of Jerusalem eleven years later.

Zedekiah was the caretaker ruler of Judah after Jehoiachin's deportation to Babylonia in the spring of 597, but legally Jehoiachin remained king. The royal properties in Judah were kept in his name, and Babylonian tablets of the period refer to him as king of Judah. Consequently, time references in the book of *Ezekiel* are often given as such and such a year or month of Jehoiachin's reign.

If you have difficulty figuring out how Ezekiel could have been in Babylon with the exiles and yet speaking face to face with people in Jerusalem, you are not alone. Many scholars are quite sure that some of his references to being physically in Babylonia were added by editors. Between Jehoiachin's exile and the final exile, Ezekiel stayed and preached in Jerusalem, but his sympathies and hopes for Israel lay with the body of Jews already taken away.

The first chapter begins with the information that it was "on the fifth day of the fifth month of the fifth year of the exile of King Jehoiachin" that Ezekiel had a vision. And it was a dandy. The inside of Ezekiel's mind had all of the scope and color and action of a "big screen" movie with the utmost in special visual effects.

"I saw it coming out of the north, a great storm cloud, with brightness all around it and lightning flashing continually in the midst of it as it roared toward me. Suddenly, out of the ominous bronze bank of cloud, four living creatures flew. They had the shape of human beings, but each had four faces, and each had four wings. Their legs were held stiff and straight and the bottoms of their feet were like the soles of calves' feet. They were the same bronze color of the cloud. Under their wings, on all four sides, they had human hands.

"They were flying in formation, with wing tips touching each other, and they came straight ahead without turning. Then I saw the faces as they came over. The face in the front of each was a human face; the face on the right side of each was that of a lion; the left-side face was like an ox; and the face in the back of each was an eagle's. They sailed on the two wings which were outstretched to touch each other, but two wings on each one covered their bodies. They could manuever in any direction without turning, as if propelled by an inner spirit.

"I looked more closely, and saw something like torches or coals of fire moving back and forth among or in the creatures. Flashes, like lightning, came out of them, and the creatures themselves could move as fast as lightning wherever they wanted to go. Coming in from the north, low to the ground, they seemed to be accompanied by wheels running on the ground below them, one wheel for each of the four. In fact, each wheel had a wheel within it, so that the wheels could go in any direction without turning. The strange wheels had spokes and rims which had eyes that looked in every direction. The wheels stayed right with the creatures. If the creatures turned right or left, the wheels turned. If the creatures rose or descended, the wheels did too. It was as if the same spirit that was in the living creatures was also in the wheels.

"Overhead the sky was like crystal, and when their wings moved it was like the sound of many waters that grew like thunder. When they stopped, they let down their wings, and as they stood still a voice came from the sky above them. Dimly seen in the brightness above them was the outline of a throne that gleamed like a sapphire. Seated above what appeared to be the throne was a likeness of a human form, from which the voice came. The upper part of the body, if you could call it that, was like bronze; the lower part of the body was like fire. The colors and brightness reminded one of an intensely brilliant rainbow.

"Instinctively, I fell on my face because I knew it was the Lord. And the voice was speaking:

" 'Son of man, stand on your feet and I will speak with you.'

"I got up, realizing that God did not want me grovelling in the dust from which Human Beings had emerged. God's Spirit helped me to my feet.

" 'Son of man, I am sending you to the people of Israel, a nation of rebels who have continued the sinful ways of their ancestors. These people are impudent and stubborn, but I am sending you to them to speak My word. Whether they hear you or refuse to hear you, when you say 'Thus says the Lord,' they will know that there is a real prophet in their midst. Don't ever be afraid of what they say or do to you; just speak My words.

" 'But you, you had better not be rebellious. Now, open your mouth and eat what I give you.'

"I looked, and I saw this hand reaching out toward me. In the hand was a scroll which it spread out before me. The writing on both front and back were words of lamentation, mourning and woe.

" 'Eat it,' the voice ordered. 'Eat this scroll and then go and speak to the house of Israel.'

"What could I do? I ate it. You know, it tasted like honey. And the voice was speaking again:

" 'Use these words when you speak to Israel. I am not sending you to a foreign land with a difficult language. Maybe if I did they would listen to you. But the house of Israel won't listen to plain speech in your own tongue. I know that because they won't listen to Me! You will just have to butt heads with them, and believe Me, they are hard-headed. However, I am going to make your head like flint. Just keep listening to Me in your heart, and keep on talking to them whether they hear or not.' "

It was the same commission Jeremiah had received a few years before, though Jeremiah's visions were brief black and white snapshots compared to the technicolor spectaculars Ezekiel reviewed.

In chapter 3, verse 12, he continues. "When the Lord was through speaking, I was aware of a noise behind me like the sound of a great earthquake, but it was the sound of the wings moving, and the wheels whirring right along with them. This time they took me with them. In my vision I was flown non-stop to Telabib, by the Chebar River in Babylonia, and when I saw our exiles there at work I sat there overwhelmed with their misery for seven days.

"At the end of seven days, I knew that the Lord was calling me to be a lookout for the people of Israel. 'When I give you the word,' the Lord said, 'you pass it on to them. If I say to the wicked you are going to die, and you don't tell them what I said, or if you don't warn them so that they may change and save their lives, then I am going to hold you responsible for what happens to them. On the other hand, if you do warn them and they still don't change, they will be in bad trouble, but you won't.

" 'The same thing is true for people who have been good people up to now. Suppose they go bad? They will have to pay for their sin, of course. But if you haven't warned them about what they are doing, then you will have to answer to Me for that. But, again, if you warn them not to sin, and they still do it, you won't be responsible. They have to take all the blame themselves.' "

It is no small thing for a person to feel that he or she has the responsibility for seeing that a whole community of people knows what is right and what is wrong. To be able to act on that responsibility without being a moral dictator who tries to manage everyone's life is quite a trick. After reading the rest of Ezekiel, you may want to say whether you think this prophet pulled it off, or not.

Chapter 3, verse 22, begins another account of Ezekiel falling on his face before the Lord. Moses was always doing that too. But once again God's Spirit lifts him up to his feet because he has to go from the plain by the Chebar River back to his home in Judah. This is the return leg of the vision journey he took to the new home of the exiles in Babylonia.

"Go home and shut yourself in your house," the Spirit told him. "Ropes will be tied on you, and you won't be able to go out among people, and I will make your tongue stick to the roof of your mouth so you can't even talk to them. When I get ready for you to speak, I will loosen your tongue and you can say, 'Anybody who wants to hear, let him/her hear; anybody who doesn't want to hear doesn't have to listen, but if you know what is good for you, you will listen.' Then tell them what I say."

"Here is one picture you can give them," the Lord told Ezekiel. "Take a lump of clay and make a miniature city like Jerusalem. Then play war. Build up a seige wall around it; build a mound up against it for bringing in the battering rams; and build a tower by the wall for shooting into the city. Between where you are sitting and the miniature city, stick up an iron plate. It will show that you, and I, are separated from the rebellious city. When anybody asks you about the exhibit, tell them that this is coming to Jerusalem.

"Here is another thing you can do after that. Take a long rest. Lie on your left side and stay there until I tell you to turn over. Every day you lie there will represent a year of the exile of Israel," the old northern kingdom. (This was not going to be any brief nap. The Lord had a rest of 390 days in mind, 13 months. If they had a *Guiness Book of Records* in those days, Ezekiel would have rewritten the record for total number of consecutive days lying on the left side we can be sure.) Everybody knew that Israel had been swept into exile by Assyria in 721 B.C., so any descendants of the original exiles of Israel had about another century and a half of exile from the old homeland to look forward to. It probably didn't worry the people of Judah who had long since forgotten about the northern kingdom anyway.

Maybe somebody kept a tally sheet on a wall outside Ezekiel's house, and every day another mark went up on the wall while the prophet lay on his left side.

"How many has he chalked up now?" people would ask each other as the days stretched out into weeks, then months. Finally, after the 390th mark went on the wall, the word went out around the city:

"He's getting up. I wonder if he can stand alone. Three hundred and ninety years—that's it for Israel."

But if Ezekiel thought he was through with the prone position for awhile, he was mistaken. No sooner had he been allowed to get off his left side than the Lord said:

"O.K., turn over. Get back on the bed and lie on your right side. This time we will show them how long Judah is going to be in exile. Set your bed out by the miniature seige of Jerusalem which you built, and face it. Have someone tie ropes around you so that you stay on your right side until I tell you the time is up."

This time the magic number was 40, and that was a number that caused a lot more interest among the citizens of Jerusalem. This number was aimed at them. With Jeremiah breaking pots, wearing wooden and iron yokes around his neck, coming out with good and bad baskets of figs, and Ezekiel acting out his sermons on the same subject, the people of Jerusalem in those days never failed to have something to talk about even if they resisted taking the messages to heart. While the citizens who watched the prophets perform might have been entertained with the stunts, these weren't exhibitions that prophets enjoyed staging. It almost makes you shudder just to read the account beginning with verse 9 of chapter 4. Ezekiel is going to have to suffer beforehand all the bad experiences he is forecasting for Jerusalem. The directions the Lord lays out are quite specific, and quite revolting:

"During the three hundred and ninety days you will be on your left side, you will carry out a number of teaching points. First, we have to show them how scarce and unappetizing eating and drinking will be when the seige comes as you have pictured it with your clay miniature. So you take wheat, barley, beans and lentils, also millet and spelt (a different kind of wheat), and mix them in one pot. Then make bread out of that mixture. That will be your food every day for the three hundred and ninety days.

"Every day?" Ezekiel must have repeated in disbelief.

"Every day. And that's not all. You will eat just once a day, and less than a pound a day. Weigh it out on the scales every day, then bake it like a barley cake over a fire made of dung, human dung. It won't be very appetizing for the people who are watching you."

"It won't be very appetizing for me either," the prophet spoke up.

"Yes, but I want you to make the point that the people of Israel will have to eat unclean bread all during their long exile among the nations."

Ezekiel was thinking quickly now. "Lord, I have never defiled myself from my childhood 'till now, never eaten anything unclean. Are You going to make me do that now?"

The Lord relented. "O.K., you can use cow dung for your fuel, but cook your bread cake every day over the cow dung."

"Less than twelve ounces (20 shekels) a day isn't much to eat, Lord."

"No, but you won't be getting any exercise, remember? And, besides, you only get one quart of water a day. That's not much to wash down dry bread."

"And, remind me, Lord, what is the point of all this?"

"We are going to show them how they will measure out bread and water during the seige—just the way you are going to do it now. And they can tell from watching you waste away how emaciated they are going to look before it is all over!"

That conversation with the Lord is hardly over when another one picks up with the beginning of chapter 5. These ideas for object-lesson sermons come so rapidly that we can't tell exactly when Ezekiel is supposed to put on the next act of his "Message From the Lord Show." He could hardly have done it while lying on either side and fasting on the one-a-day mixed grain biscuits, so let's figure that he is now up and around again.

"Son of man, (that's the Lord's favorite name for Ezekiel) I want you to take a sharp sword, a real sharp one, and use it for a barber's razor. Cut off your hair, and cut off your beard." (This business is making a wreck out of Ezekiel slowly but surely.) "Take your balances that you used to weigh out your bread ration every day and weigh your hair, then divide it into three parts. Make sure that everyone knows you have cut your hair. There won't be any point to doing all this if people aren't paying attention."

"What do I do with the hair after I get it cut and divided into thirds?" the prophet, who is now surprised at nothing, asked.

"Take the first third and make a show of burning it right in the middle of the city. After you do that, take the second part and go around the city throwing it up and swinging at it with the sword. Finally, scatter the rest of your hair in a strong wind. Keep a little of this last handful and tie it up in your robe. When everybody gathers around to discuss the meaning of all this with you, you can take a little part of the hair you saved and burn it. While their attention is riveted on it, make this speech, just the way I am giving it to you:

"This is from the Lord God. You are worse than the nations around you. You have done more to be disobedient to My commandments than any of them. In fact, you have paid more attention to trying to ape their ordinances and laws than you have to Mine. So I am going to punish you right in the midst of the nations so that everyone can see what happens when this nation turns away from its God. I am going to be harder on you than I have ever been before, or ever will be again. What could be worse than starvation which drives parents to eat their own children, and children to eat their parents? You have defiled My sanctuary and the whole land with your filthy idols and images, and since you have completely forsaken Me, I will forsake you completely.

"Here is what I was doing with the three parts of my hair. The third that I burned in the city center represents the third of Jerusalem's people who will die of famine and disease in the city. The third that was hacked with the sword represents another third of the people who will die by the sword in the invasion. And the last third God will scatter in exile the way the hair blew away with the wind. All that will be left is a ruin that will remind any who pass by of the Lord's vengeance. From now on, people will make each other shudder just by mentioning what God is going to do to Jerusalem."

Note to reader: Don't look for any intermission between the acts of this drama. When one scene is concluded, the next one moves onstage without even a set change. So chapter 6 starts right in with another idea from the Lord:

"Son of man, I want you to make a speech to the hills around the city. Get a crowd out in the open and shake your fist toward the hilltops, and say 'Listen, you mountains and valleys, God is going to destroy all the false worship places on you. All your incense altars will be burned up, and all your idols will be cut down along with the worshippers who will be slain all around you. There will be nothing left of your so-called 'sacred places' except dry bones.' "

"Will everybody be wiped out, Lord?"

"No, you can always promise them that a few will escape death. They will be taken away captive to other nations, and there they will have time to reflect on all this. There they will know that I have done what I said I would. Then clap your hands and stamp your foot, and cry out loud, 'O, it is going to be so terrible! All these people dying by the sword, or pestilence, or famine because of these stupid abominable idols everywhere!' "

Likewise, chapter 7 quickly follows:

"Here's another one, Son of man. The end is drawing near since the army of Nebuchadrezzar approaches. Really stick it to them. Tell them that all the disaster you have been warning them about is finally at hand. That 'day of the Lord' their false prophets liked to talk about is here. It will be the Lord's Day all right, the Lord's day to punish for all your wicked ways. It is a day of doom, no mercy, no pity! The days of 'business as usual' are over; there won't be any buying or selling because there won't be anything left to buy or sell. You can throw your gold and silver in the street; there isn't a thing it can buy you now, and starving people can't eat their precious metals. Because you thought material wealth was more important than anything else in your world, you made it your god. You literally made it your god by fashioning it into idols. Now they can't even save themselves, much less you. Foreigners will take them all away, and the Lord will turn away and take no notice that they are defiling even the holy temple before they destroy it.

"There is absolutely nothing anyone can do to stop the terror that is coming. And God is saying 'they asked for it; they wouldn't believe My word that such judgment would come; and now they are going to get it!' "

The Glory Departs

Ezekiel's next vision, in chapter 8, has a date on it. This one came before the lying on the side and cutting off the hair episodes, actually only a little more than a year after his first vision in which he was called to be a prophet at thirty years of age. It is the sixth year, the sixth month, and the fifth day of Jehoiachin's exile. He was already accepted enough as a prophet to be consulted by some of the elders of the nation. While they were seated there with him in his house he went into a trance. In it he saw the form, like a human being in shape, with fire from the waist down and bronze radiance from the waist up. This spirit form took him by the hair of the head and lifted him up for a trip over to the entrance of the north gate of the temple of Jerusalem.

"I want you to see this," the Spirit form said. "Look at this fertility cult worship going on right here in this court of the temple which was erected to the Lord God. Look at that image of the goddess, Asherah, standing in the entrance just north of the altar gate! Do you see what they are doing to drive Me away from My own house? But I will show you worse than that."

Now he was looking down at the door of a court that had been sealed off years before. There was a hole in the wall.

"Dig in that hole and enlarge it, and tell me what you see," the Spirit said.

Lo and behold! There was a doorway. People could slip in and out of the room.

"Go on in," the Spirit said, "and see the vile abominations people are committing in this place."

Cautiously he entered, and there on the walls were the same pictures of reptiles and animals you would see in worship chambers in Egypt. All the idols that were supposed to have been destroyed a few years back in Josiah's reformation were placed around the room, and through the haze of smoke from the incense pots Ezekiel could see seventy Jewish elders engaging in this pagan worship. One of them he identified as Jaazaniah, a son of Shaphan, the secretary to former King Josiah, who went to Huldah for the word that began the reform movement that did away with these foreign images his son now worshipped again. Here in the "underground" the party, now outlawed, which wanted an alliance with Egypt still was thriving. Before many years they would be strong enough to openly press the caretaker king, Zedekiah, to revolt against Babylon, with the thought that Egypt would protect Judah.

"See what they are doing in the dark," the Spirit said. "But you haven't seen it all yet. Come on."

Next stop for Ezekiel in this vision trip was an area of the temple court where a whole bunch of women sat weeping for Tammuz, a god, originally from Sumeria, who was supposed to die each fall and come to life each spring.

"Yes, that's bad," the Spirit answered Ezekiel's thought, "but this is worse. Look here inside the inner court of God's House, at the very door of the temple sanctuary. See those twenty-five men with their backs to the sanctuary and facing east? You know what they are doing? Worshipping the sun!"

Ezekiel was shocked.

"All this right in the House of the Lord of Israel! Now

you see why I will have to deal with them, and I will have no pity. They turn their backs literally on My Presence; they thumb their noses at Me. No matter how loud they cry when disaster falls on them, I won't hear them!"

Then the Spirit form turned and called loudly (though only Ezekiel could hear and see),

"Come near, you executioners. Bring your weapons of death in your hands."

Six men came from the direction of the upper gate (judgment ought to begin in the temple or church). Each one had an executioner's ax in his hand. And along with them came another, clothed in white linen, with a writing case at his side. They all went into the sanctuary and stood by the bronze altar.

Ezekiel sensed that the unseen God of the altar had now moved over to the threshold of the entrance and was calling the man in the linen suit to come over there. These were the instructions the Lord gave to him:

"Go out into the city and put a mark on the forehead of every person who really feels badly that all this false worship is going on among them." Then the other six, the executioners, were given this order:

"Follow him around, and kill every person, old or young, male or female, who does not have a mark on the forehead. Begin right here in My sanctuary."

They did. They killed everybody in the temple and left the dead bodies to defile the sacred area. Then they went out into the city to keep on slaughtering. By now Ezekiel is sick, even though this is just a vision. He fell on his face (Ezekiel is overtaking Moses in the contest to see who falls on the face the most), and he cried out in protest:

"Ah, Lord God! Are You going to destroy all that remains of Israel in this burst of wrath against Jerusalem?"

God came right back with the answer. "They have been

filling My land with injustice while they were saying 'The Lord does not see.' So I'm not looking now; they have to pay!''

Just then the man with the briefcase came back to report. "I have done what You told me to do."

Immediately, (chapter 10) Ezekiel's attention is drawn back to the space above the altar above the carved cherubim. A brilliant sapphire throne appeared there, and from it the divine Voice was speaking again to the man in the linen suit:

"Go in among the whirling wheels (Ezekiel's props seemed always in motion) beneath the cherubim. Fill your hands with burning coals you will find there, and then scatter them all over the city." The cherubim were standing on the south side of the room, and from that area came a dense cloud almost too brilliant to look at. It filled the court of the temple, and the sound of the whirring wings of the cherubim could be heard as far as the outer court.

The man in linen went in and stood beside a wheel beneath the cherubim. An angel stretched out a hand from between the cherubim and took some of the burning coals to hand to the man who turned and left the temple with it.

It was then that Ezekiel noticed a wheel beside each of the four cherubs, bright, translucent wheels. Like the ones he had seen in his first vision, each wheel had another wheel inside it, set crosswise so that the wheels could go in any direction without having to change anything. The wheel in front of the line of four always led the others. These wheels had eyes all over their spokes and rims also. Ezekiel heard someone call them "the whirling wheels," which they certainly were, though they might have been called the "face wheels." Each one of them somehow had four faces. The vision teller did not pause to say just where they were located or attached, if they were. But each set of four faces included a face of a cherub, a face of a human being, a face of a lion, and a face of an eagle.

"So," Ezekiel said to himself, "these are the living creatures that I saw in the first vision. The wheels go everywhere the cherubim go, and all are directed by the living Spirit within them. And now they are going to be the vehicle which carries the glory of the Lord away from this temple." The glory of the Lord hovered over the cherubim wheels as it paused by the east gate of the temple. Then it took off straight ahead.

No more would the Presence of God be found in the great temple!

Later, probably during the seige days when the Babylonians were attacking the city, the Spirit ushered Ezekiel back to the temple, to the east gate of the inner court. He got there in time to find twenty-five of the leading princes of the government. Two of them are named, Jaazaniah and Pelatiah. They are the core of the group who have been giving bad advice to the king, and had resisted the message of prophets like Jeremiah and Ezekiel that these days of doom were coming.

"The walls of this city are like a cauldron, and we are the meat in it," they were saying.

"No," Ezekiel interrupts, "Thus says the Lord: 'all the people you have caused to be killed with your corrupt counsel, they are the real meat in this pressure cooker. They will suffer for it. But you will not die here. You will be taken away, you who fear the sword so much, and at the border of Israel you will meet your judgment. There you will realize that I am the Lord you should have obeyed!' "

While he was speaking, Pelatiah fell down dead. Perhaps startled by such an immediate effect of his prediction, Ezekiel then fell on his face again and exclaimed to the Lord, "Ah, Lord God! Are You going to make a complete end of the remnant of Israel?"

"Son of man, don't be so upset. Think a minute. These people have been saying that your brothers and sisters already in exile have gone too far away for Me to be interested in them anymore. Well, I haven't forgotten them. Actually, I am taking care of them, and someday I will gather a remnant from them and return them to Israel. When they get back they will remove all traces of these abominable worship practices which I hate. I will change their stony hearts to soft hearts, and they will be people of My own heart. But, as for these people here, whose hearts go out after detestable things, I will let them pay for their deeds. Don't worry about them."

Here, beginning with verse 22 of chapter 11, the cherubim-and-wheels outfit now takes off and takes the glory of the Lord out of the temple, out of the city, to rest on a mountain to the east. And Ezekiel pictures himself being transported again to Babylon where he told the exiles that the Lord had said they were going to be the remnant saved for rebuilding Judah.

Jeremiah's word to the exiles was similar, as we have read, but Jeremiah never pictured the Presence of the Lord as leaving the temple, or anywhere else. H.B. may try to ignore the Presence of God, but she/he can never leave God's Presence, simply because there is no place where God is not. Ezekiel knew that too. His vivid word pictures only served, he hoped, to underscore that growing alienation from God the leaders and people of Jerusalem were causing with their sin.

Jeremiah walked around with a yoke on his shoulders to picture the coming exile. Ezekiel worked the streets too.

"Get yourself a knapsack and fill it with the stuff you would take if you were being forced to hit the road as a captive of Babylon," the Lord told him. "Make sure everybody sees you with the exile baggage. Then, at evening, go over to a wall and make a hole in it. Explain that it represents the wall of the city which will be broken down by the enemy. Lift your baggage through that hole and go out the other side into the darkness. Put a blindfold over your eyes for effect maybe. These people are so hard of hearing! Maybe they will get the point from your pantomine."

Ezekiel did that, perhaps more than once.

"This will get their attention," the Lord said. "Now when they ask 'why are you doing this?' you tell them that I said that this concerns the king's household. What you have done they are going to do, only for real. They will be forced to take up their bags and leave in the night, and they will cover their eyes because they won't want to look at the land they are leaving. I will take the king to Babylon, where he will die, but he won't ever be able to see it.

"The rest of the people here I will scatter to the four winds, the few who escape from death by the sword or famine. There they can confess among the other nations the terrible evils they did here to bring My judgment upon themselves."

Here's another one Ezekiel was encouraged by the Lord to try (12:17-20).

"Learn how to eat your bread with shaking hand, and when you drink let your hand tremble as if you are afraid. When people notice it, tell them that they will eat and drink with fright when they see their land being stripped because of the unfaithfulness of the people here. Remind them again that this land is going to be a wasteland, so they will remember that I am God."

"But after I have been preaching the same 'destruction is coming' sermon for years, and old Jeremiah has been preaching it a lot longer than I have, how do I answer the smart people who say 'We have been waiting a long time, but none of your visions have come true yet?' "

"Just tell them," the Lord said, "that the end is coming soon now. You will see it in your own days. I am getting ready to close out this deal."

Always a complicating factor in the reception given, or not given, to the true prophets was the preaching of the false prophets. They kept saying what the people wanted to hear, that everything would be O.K. with Judah; no need to worry.

"Woe to these preachers who have never contacted the Lord! They just speak out of their own minds, and they lie when they say the Lord sent them. They are like foxes or jackals among the ruins, never doing anything themselves to build up the moral defense of the city. Things are going to destruction around them and they don't even know it. They think that if they preach 'peace and prosperity' long enough, God will have to make it happen.

" 'I am going to weed them out,' the Lord says. 'These prophets see a crack in the wall, and instead of revealing it they daub whitewash over it and pretend it isn't there. Well, a big rain is coming with hail and strong wind. Not only will the whitewash wash away, the whole wall will fall. Then let us see them whitewash that! They won't be around to whitewash anything anymore, because the walls will fall on them.'

"Don't you be caught up in that, son of man," the Lord continued. "And don't go easy on the women prophets who take fees for speaking words of 'peace.' Especially speak out against those women sorcerers who practice 'black magic,' claiming they can cause the death of enemies (for a fee) by tying on magic wrist bands or veils, or by doing those things to guarantee safety and good health for the payer. That is real blasphemy, pretending they can usurp powers that belong only to God.

"Tell them that God is going to tear the bands and veils off them, and that God is going to protect the righteous from any such intimidation from them. Their sorcery and fortune telling never challenges a wicked person to change his or her ways. That is the mark of true prophecy!"

With whom is a true prophet supposed to talk anyway? That question comes to Ezekiel's mind, as related in chapter 14. Some elders who were thoroughly sold on the worship of their idols came to inquire of the Lord's word one day. Would God even speak to them?

"Yes, of course I will," the Lord assured Ezekiel. "I am eager to lay hold on the souls of all My people who have been estranged from Me through their worship of idols. My word to them is clear: 'Repent. Turn away from your idols. If any person comes to Me and still puts his or her idols ahead of me, then I will cut that person off and not count that person as one of My people anymore. If the prophet says anything less definite, or more hopeful, than that, I will cut the prophet off too. This idol worship has got to stop once and for all. Period.' "

There was more. "When a land deliberately goes against Me and I decide to act to punish it, I don't care if Noah, Daniel (not the famous Daniel of a later lion's den) and Job all lived there, I would strike everybody but them. Their righteousness couldn't save the others. If I send wild beasts to ravage the land, they will kill all the unfaithful. The goodness of these three couldn't protect anybody but themselves. If I send the sword to strike them down, or pestilence to wipe them out, nothing could stop the total destruction. And this is just what Jerusalem is going to get—the terrible four: sword, famine, wild beasts, and pestilence. If there are any survivors to be led away into exile, everyone will be able to see from watching them that My punishment of Israel was fully justified. If there is any consolation in that, you can have it."

Move into chapter 15. Start it off by thinking about grape vines. The wood isn't very good wood. "Offhand," the Lord says to Ezekiel, "I can't think of any lower-grade wood in the forest. It isn't good enough for anyone to make a peg to hang a kettle on. People burn it for fuel, and when it is burned it is worth even less, of course. Now, if it was useless when it was whole, how much more useless is it after it is burned? That is just exactly how much value this city is going to have after it is burned to the ground. It is worthless now; it will be even more worthless then."

"Think about the history of this place anyway," the Lord says in 16. "You could use that history by saying that I, the Lord, think of Jerusalem this way:

"Your origin was in the land of Canaan. Your father was an Amorite and your mother a Hittite, the people who settled the land at that time. When you were born, nobody took care of you. Your naval string was not tied off; you were never washed and wrapped in soft cloth. They cast you out into the open field because nobody wanted you.

"I passed by and saw you there, and I wanted you to live so I saved you. You grew up, a tall young woman, fully developed and mature, but still naked in the desert. When I passed by you again, I noticed that you were ready for love, so I made the marriage covenant with you and you became My wife. I gave you everything you needed, new clothes, shoes, jewelry, and a beautiful crown on your head. You had the finest things to eat, and gradually you became an elegant woman of the world. Everywhere in the other nations, they spoke of your beauty and the perfection which I gave you.

"But your beauty went to your head and you played the harlot with other lovers. You took some of the bright garments which I gave you Myself and decorated shrines where you entertained other suitors. You took the jewels and gold and silver which were presents from Me and made for yourself images of men. You set My oil and My incense before them. The flour, oil, and honey which I left for your appetite you put before them as offerings. You even took the sons and daughters you had borne to Me and sacrificed them on those despicable altars, or burned them alive. Has anything ever been seen like it? Never once have you remembered the days of your childhood and youth when you were bloody and naked, without clothes or food!

"As if that were not enough, you began to build temples for prostitution all over town, places where you played the cult prostitute in the name of worship. Like a lustful harlot you ran after the Egyptians, looking to Egypt for aid in time of trouble instead of to Me. So I allowed part of your property to be taken by the Philistines, but the warning escaped you. Still your lust was not satisfied, so you played the harlot with the Assyrians, and then later with the Babylonians. And even now you are not satisfied.

"How brazen can a prostitute get? Yet you were not exactly a prostitute, because you didn't do it for money or pay. No, you were the adulterous wife receiving strangers instead of her husband. Men give gifts to harlots, but you gave gifts to them to get them to come to you. Your shame has no bounds; so here is what I am finally going to do to you:

"I will gather all your lovers from every side, all the nations from around, and invite them to see how good you look without your finery. I will let them do what they want with you. They will tear down the temples and the shrines where you prostituted yourself for other gods. They will destroy your buildings and take away all your wealth. They will leave you naked and bare, cut up with their swords, with no houses left. And My jealousy will be satisfied. I will calm down, perhaps. But all of this is coming to you because you have forgotten the days of your youth and the covenant you made with Me.

"You know what proverb everybody uses with you now? "Like mother, like daughter." You are the daughter of your mother who loathed her husband and her children. You are truly the sister of your sisters who left their husbands and children too. Your mother was a Hittite and your father an Amorite, and your sister is Samaria who lived to the north of you, and your younger sister who lived to the south of you is Sodom. The trouble is that you were even worse than they, more corrupt in all your ways. Your sister, Sodom, and her daughters, had too much pride, too much prosperity and ease, but did not aid the poor and needy. They were haughty and did terrible things, so I removed them. And Samaria looks virtuous beside you. Samaria was destroyed for half the sins you have committed.

"Someday I will restore Sodom and Samaria, and even you. Meanwhile, remember how Sodom was a byword with you for evil and corruption? That was before your own guilt was uncovered. Now the daughters of Edom and Philistia and the other nations around you use you as an illustration of the worst they can imagine. Still, someday I will establish again the covenant we knew in the days of your youth. Then you will remember and be ashamed, and we will let bygones be bygones."

On With The Show

Remember, there is no necessary sequence to these visions and "words from the Lord." So when chapter 17 opens with an entirely different approach from God to Ezekiel, we are not surprised.

"Son of man, give them a riddle the next time you speak in public. Try this one:

"A great eagle with massive, beautiful wings came to Lebanon and broke the top right out of a cedar tree. He took the topmost branch and carried it to a land of traders. He set it down in the city of merchants. Then he took the seed of the land and planted it in good soil, and watered it well. The seed grew to be a low-spreading vine which stayed rooted where it was planted but it spread its branches out toward the eagle.

"But there was another great eagle with massive wings and beautiful plumage, and the vine turned one day to shoot its branches out toward the new eagle for watering. The second eagle took the vine from the bed where it was planted and transplanted it to another location, hoping it would become a noble vine.

"Now the question for you to ask them is this: will the transplanted vine thrive, or will it wither away when the hot east wind blows on it? While they are thinking about an answer, you give it to them. The king of Babylon came to Jerusalem and took her king and princes back to Babylon. Then he took one of the royal seed and planted him here to be in power as long as he obeyed Babylon. But the newly-planted king rebelled, turning to Egypt for military help. Will he succeed? Can he break the covenant he made with the king of Babylon? Pharaoh will help with no mighty army when Babylon builds the seige mounds against this city, like the hot wind from the east. The king will die in Babylon.

"It's the covenant with God that he has broken, and it is God Who will see that Zedekiah's army is broken, his people scattered, and he, himself, will be taken captive to Babylon for judgment. Then God will take a sprig from the top of a lofty cedar and set it out on a high mountain. It will grow to be a great cedar and under it the animals will come to live. In its branches many kinds of birds will build their nests. When they see it on the height of Israel, the other trees will know that the Lord can bring a high tree low, or make a low tree high. The Lord can dry up a green tree or make a dry tree flourish."

(If he didn't actually name the king, or even offer his explanation of the riddle in public, could Ezekiel have been convicted of treason by the government? At least one other prophet, Uriah, had lost his life, and Jeremiah had been thrown down a well because they named names when they preached. Ezekiel had to watch his step. He did, and in some of his ideas he was a step ahead of other thinkers of his time. Theologians of the Jewish-Christian tradition have always regarded his insights revealed in chapter 18 as one of his big contributions to our thought. He was thinking one day about the proverb often used and accepted by Jewish teachers: "The parents have eaten wild grapes, and the children's teeth are set on edge." And he heard the Lord say, "Cut it. Quit using that line of thought. Every individual soul is Mine; the soul that sins will die for its own sins, not for somebody elses."

The Lord went on to lead Ezekiel's thoughts: "If a person is righteous, if that person does not go after idols, does not break the commandments about relationships with other people, doesn't hurt anyone, but, on the other hand, helps all he/she can, that person will live abundantly. Now, if that parent has a child who is a bad one who breaks all the rules, will the parent's credit keep the child from dying? No. The child has to answer for himself or herself.

"Go one step further. Suppose this bad child has a child who sees all the sins of the parent and decides to be good, then that person shall surely live. But this proverb of yours says that the good child should suffer because of the bad parent's sins. That's ridiculous. Every person has to be accountable for his or her own sin. The good person finds life; the evil person finds death. But, even beyond that, if a sinful person repents and changes to be a person who does right, then that person will live. The past sins will be forgotten, and the present goodness will be accepted. I don't have any pleasure in the death of the wicked. I would much rather they turned and took the way of life."

Ezekiel must have been wondering: "Then how about a righteous person (or nation) who turns away from the good life and becomes wicked?" And the answer came: "That person has chosen death. Isn't that just and fair? Why are people in the House of Israel saying that the Lord is not just? Don't they have that backward? It is their ways that are not just. So I will judge every person according to his or her own ways."

Armed with that assurance, Ezekiel could make an altar call at the end of every sermon: "Repent! Cast off your present way of thinking and acting. Get yourself a new heart and a new spirit! Why will you die, House of Israel? The

Lord has no pleasure in the death of anyone. So turn, and live! Turn, and live!''

The lamentation, or funeral dirge poem, which makes up chapter 19 breaks up the prose visions nicely. Yet it is another way of getting across the point that exile is coming.

"Judah was a lioness with young lions to rear. One of her young ones became a young lion who learned how to catch prey, even to devour people. But he was captured and taken away in chains to another land.

"The lioness took another one of her whelps and taught him to be a fierce lion who devoured his prey. He ravaged the land all around, and many people were terrified at the sound of his roaring. Then enemies set snares for him, finally caged him and took him to meet the king of Babylon. No more will his voice be heard among the hills of Israel.'' (Scholars disagree as to whether the first young lion was Jehoahaz, immediate successor to Josiah, who was taken to Egypt, or Jehoiakim who was the ruler when Babylon first attacked Jerusalem, or Jehoiachin who ruled the last three months before the first exile. But Zedekiah was the second lion who was going to be caged and deported, and that was the point of the lament. It was the same theme the prophets had been playing in so many ways.)

The second part of the poetic lament changes the picture, but not the message.

"Judah is like a vine in a vineyard, well watered, full of branches and fruit. Its tallest stem towered above the others, high above the thick branches. And since it stuck up in its pride, the hot east wind scorched it, dried up its fruit, and withered it till fire consumed it. (The stem of David's line, once so proud and lofty above the rest of Israel, is going to be cut down and destroyed by the fire from the east, Babylon.) It will be transplanted in Babylon, but in the new desert home there will be no strong stem to rule over it."

Again, in the tenth day of the fifth month of the seventh year of Jehoiachin's exile, some elders of Israel were at Ezekiel's door, wanting to know what the Lord's latest word might be. It was this:

"Son of man, ask the elders of Israel if they have really come to inquire of Me. I have nothing more to say to them than what you have been saying: the abominations of your people and yourselves are killing you. I swore to their ancestors before I brought them out of the slavery of Egypt that I would make a covenant with them and bring them into a good land which I had promised to them. I told them to throw away the idols and images of other gods which they had picked up in Egypt. But they never did it; they wouldn't give up their idols. I should have taken it out on them right there, but I didn't think the other nations would interpret that as My caring for them. So I brought them out of Egypt so the nations could see that I was saving them.

"In the wilderness I showed them My laws for living, laws for all H.B.s. I set up the sabbath idea as a perpetual reminder of My continuing renewal of them. But do you think that they obeyed My commands or kept My ordinances? They stubbornly refused. They wouldn't even keep the sabbaths which I designed for their own comfort. So I kept them away from the Promised Land for years, thinking that they would repent. It crossed My mind to wipe them out, but I decided not to do it. Perhaps the next generation would see the light and keep the covenant, I figured. Wrong again! They were no better than their parents. And none of the generations of Israel since have obeyed My commandments any better.

"Now, let's get down to cases. Is this present bunch any more willing to follow Me than their parents have been? No, they still make their sacrifices to idols and false gods, even to the repulsive point of burning their own children! And yet they come to hear some comforting word from Me? Tell them that it is back to the wilderness for them. This time I am sending them out into a wilderness of nations, scattering those who survive among them.

"So let Israel go right on serving the idols, but they can stop profaning My name with their gifts and their false worship. There will come a time when some of them will return to this mountain to worship Me with their whole hearts, and with all their talents and gifts. And I will accept them, and bless them as a sign to all the nations. They will know then that I am the God who made the covenant with them, and Who keeps My part of the covenant no matter what they have done to break theirs." (20:1-44)

Back in chapter 6, Ezekiel made a speech to the mountains and hills. In that instance he was facing north. The little speech is misplaced, and should be right here in chapter 20, because in verses 45-49 he now turns and faces south with a similar brief sermon. Maybe he was standing on the Mount of Olives or some high point so that he could see north, then south, and then (in chapter 21) back toward the city of Jerusalem.

"I am looking at you," Ezekiel says to the hill country covered with trees to the south of the city (not to the Negeb which was desert country farther south). "I see trees now, but a fire is coming to burn every green tree and every dry tree. And everybody around will be singed by the fire the Lord brings." He says it, by the Lord's direction, but then pauses to make an aside to the Lord, "You know, they think I can only speak in allegories, never saying anything straight out!"

"Well, make the speech toward Jerusalem a little plainer," the Lord must have whispered back. Because nobody could miss the meaning of his speech in chapter 21.

"The Lord is taking the sword from the sheath, and everybody in your city is going to get cut down, the good and the bad."

God said, "Sigh when you say it. Sigh with a breaking heart and weeping eyes. And when they ask you why you sigh, you say 'because I am seeing the terrible catastrophe which is coming on you. When it comes you will all faint and tremble!' "

If a sigh won't get their attention, perhaps a sword will. So the prophet wields a sword, a polished sword, showing how sharp it is and ready for cutting.

"This is the sword of the Lord, ready to be used by the slayer who comes against us. All the leaders and people of our land are being delivered to their fate. You have not learned when God chastened you with a rod. Now comes the sword, cutting to the right and left, once, twice, three times, swift as lightning."

"Make it even plainer," the Lord told Ezekiel. "Mark out two ways for the sword of the king of Babylon to come. Put up signposts at an intersection. On one of them put an arrow 'To Rabah (in Ammon)'; on the other 'To Judah and Jerusalem.' The king of Babylon now stands at that intersection and must decide by divination which of the two rebellious countries to attack first. He is going to play 'spin the arrow,' also consult his idols, and then read the liver of a sacrificed animal (like reading tea leaves). Everything is going to point to Jerusalem, and he will come to attack this city."

"Hot air! Rubbish!" some of his hearers reacted.

"Because you won't admit your sins, you will be overtaken in them," the prophet shouted. And you, unanointed king of Judah, the time for your final punishment has come. Take off that turban and crown. It doesn't belong to you. Wearing it doesn't make you a king in Jehoiachin's place!

You and everything here that is high are going to be brought low. This place will be a ruin, without a trace, and it will be that until God gives the crown to the one who has a right to wear it!''

(If Jeremiah spoke plainly to Zedekiah face to face, then Ezekiel would join him in open defiance of the caretaker king whose rebellion, along with Ammon, was bringing the Babylonian army back to destroy them all.)

''The same thing is going to happen to the Ammonites, of course. Whether Nebuchadrezzar comes to Jerusalem first, or through Ammon first, their fate is sealed the same as ours. They will be burned and slaughtered, wiped out, never to be a nation again.''

Chapter 22 relates another sermon to Jerusalem which the Lord urged Ezekiel to preach.

''What shall we expect for a city where innocent people are killed, and where idols are worshipped? Your appointed time has come, and God's punishment of you will be a shock to many nations. The government is guilty of murders of innocent citizens; parents are treated with contempt instead of honor; foreigners are cheated and oppressed, and widows and orphans are mistreated. You have despised the keeping of the sabbath and other laws of the Lord, and many people here commit acts of lewdness without shame; no woman is safe from violation. Bribes and extortion are accepted as ways of doing business. . . the list could go on and on.

''See me strike my hands together? That is the way the Lord is going to smash us and send us out to be filtered through the nations until we are made clean. It will be embarrassing to our God for all the world to see this, but you shall know that the Lord is God.

''You know how mineral ore has to be put into the furnace and fired in order to melt away the dross from the precious metal, like silver or gold? Well, you are so dross that God is going to have to melt you in the midst of the fire to see if there is anything worth saving."

Another sermon, beginning with verse 23, deplores the violence of the leaders of government toward the people, and the looseness of the leaders of the church who have not taught the people any respect for God or sacred things. To make matters worse, the prophets, who are supposed to blow the whistle on such evils in state and church, do a whitewash job on the whole business. God has looked in vain for even one person who would be upright enough that God would save the land. So disaster must come.

"You've heard the one about the two sisters who acted as prostitutes in Egypt?"

That was an opening line designed to catch the attention of the audience (chapter 23).

"As young women they allowed themselves to be fondled. Oholah was the older one, and Oholibah her sister. Oholah is Samaria, and Oholibah is Jerusalem. Both were married to the Lord, and both produced sons and daughters. But Oholah became a lover of the Assyrians who were so handsome and mighty. She defiled herself with their idols, and practiced the same harlotry she had engaged in as a young woman in Egypt. So the Lord let her lovers, the Assyrians, have her. They took her, mistreated her, and killed her and her sons and daughters.

"The younger sister, Ohalibah, saw all this happen, yet she was even more of a prostitute at heart than Samaria had been. She went after the Assyrian men too, and then she saw pictures of the intriguing men of Babylonia. All of them looked like dashing officers to her. So she sent for them and they came to pollute her with their lust. Soon she tired of them, but the Lord had already given her up in disgust also. Now the Babylonians will be allowed to do to her what the Assyrians did to her sister. (Since children may be reading this chapter, we won't repeat here the terrible description of what will happen to the Jerusalem sister, given in verses 25-35.)

Anyway, it is the task of the true prophet, as Ezekiel sees it, to make the judgment of God plain to the offending sister, Jerusalem or Oholibah. When the people of Judah are giving their love and attention to idols, it is like a wife or husband being unfaithful to the marriage. It is nothing less than religious adultery, adultery of the grossest kind, adultery of the spirit or soul. Then, when some even add child sacrifice in their adulterous acts with false gods, the horrible shame of it is compounded.

Politically, the nation plays the harlot when it invites envoys of foreign nations to ask favors from them. Israel's God is perfectly capable of protecting and guiding the Chosen People. When the nation makes entangling alliances with other nations (Egypt, Assyria, Babylon, whoever), it betrays her lack of trust in the Lord God. These new "lovers" will only abuse her in the end. Any "righteous" people who can think clearly still will condemn her as the adulteress she is. She will also be held guilty of murder, because her lovers have the blood of innocent people on their hands. At best, she is a willing accomplice; at worst, she is a murderer as well as a whore.

"This is why you are going to be punished with terror and slaughter and fire," Ezekiel stated often to Jerusalem. All the rest of chapter 23 he made the description of that punishment unbearably plain.

On the tenth day of the tenth month of the ninth year of Jehoiachin's exile, the Babylonian army finally arrived to begin the final seige of Jerusalem. And the Lord told Ezekiel to announce, in effect, "things are really cooking now!" So the prophet found a rusty cooking pot, probably a castoff copper vessel priests no longer used because it was too corroded to be cleaned, and he set it over a hot fire which he built in the street. Into it he put a good many pieces of meat and bones. All the while he was singing a little cooking song that he adapted for his purposes (24:3-5).

"While you are cooking this mess," the Lord said, "take out an occasional piece of meat at random, and say that only a few will be taken alive from the rusty, bloody pot which is Jerusalem. Tell them I am making the fire bigger (while you pile on more wood). When it is boiling over, tip the water out of it and leave the pot on the fire till all the meat and bones are burned up. Then leave the empty pot on the hot coals until the copper itself melts. Tell them that God got weary of trying to clean the rust from the filthy Jerusalem pot (Josiah's scrubbing reform only touched the surface), and now the whole pot has to be destroyed."

"And that," Ezekiel said to the onlookers as the pot was burned completely, "is exactly what is going to happen to this city before the Babylonians are through with it!" What a wonderful "call to arms" that was on the first day of an enemy attack! Jeremiah is standing on one corner advising everybody to carry a white flag and go surrender to the enemy, and Ezekiel is on another burning a pot and saying "this is how much chance we have of winning." Is it any wonder that the government leaders who were madly deploying their defense forces to repel the Babylonian assault considered the prophets as less than helpful in the defense effort?

Even the deepest of personal tragedies was taken by the prophet as a sign from the Lord, a sign to be used in pressing home the one-theme sermon of his life. Ezekiel's wife was at the point of death (24:15-27), and the Lord prepared him for the blow. "It will be hard on you, but I don't want you to show any emotion in public, nor do I want you to do any of the ordinary things a husband does at the time of his wife's death. You will cry in private, of course, but publicly you will not shed a tear. Get up the next morning, put your hat on your head, your shoes on your feet, and don't wear black or any sign of mourning. When people bring food to the house as acts of sympathy and grief, tell them you are going about business as usual today."

One morning Ezekiel preached a sermon; that evening his wife died. With only one night of private grief and adjustment, the faithful husband and prophet of the Lord rose the next morning to do what the Lord had bidden. He dressed for going out into the city, with his regular attire for speaking to the people. Knowing of the death of his wife, people who saw him found it hard to understand what he was doing. They asked him, as the Lord knew they would:

"What's this you are doing? Your wife just died and you are acting as if nothing has happened. Instead of staying home for the days of mourning, you are dressed as if you are ready to go on a trip somewhere."

"Exactly," the prophet replied. "Remember this when you look at me. God is going to take away the temple, the pride of your life, as my wife was the pride of mine. Your sons and daughters and families who are left behind will be killed. But you should keep your hats and shoes on, because you will be marched away captive, with no time for mourning. Only to yourselves will you show your distress and grief."

The last two verses of chapter 24 don't fit here at all. But if you look back to chapter 3:24 you find the beginning of the little story where this does fit. The prophet was told to stay in his house, bound up, until further notice from the Lord. It is probable that, after his recent speeches at the beginning of the seige, he was arrested as Jeremiah was. Forced to stay in his house (possibly outside the city), and perhaps even bound with ropes, he had to wait until the day the city finally fell. Then a refugee ("fugitive") would bring the news. He would then be free, of course, to speak again.

The Ammonites were in this cauldron too. They had agreed with Zedekiah to try to throw off the authority of Babylon. So they were also the object of this western sweep of the Babylonian armies. In chapter 25, Ezekiel has words for them as well.

"You are laughing now because Israel has been destroyed, and the temple profaned and leveled! You won't be laughing long. The same destroyer from the east has you marked up next on his timetable. The same forces will be eating your fruit, drinking your milk, and making your cities into pastures for their flocks. When it happens, just remember that this is the judgment of God upon you for your malice toward Israel!"

Unfinished Business

Following his swipe at the Ammonites, Ezekiel continues with prophecies concerning all the other neighboring countries, just as Jeremiah did. The two reinforced each other at every point.

"Moab is going to catch it, along with Ammon," Ezekiel warned. "And Edom, which made a show of taking revenge on Judah when the Babylonians had Judah down, is going to be laid low as well.

"The same goes for the Philistines, long-time enemies of Judah.

"And Tyre, which thought that Judah's defeat opened a door of opportunity for it to expand, is going to be washed away in a tide of conquest, much like the waves of the sea break on its shores."

A good bit of space is given to Tyre. Ezekiel, no doubt, foresaw Nebuchadrezzar's ultimate victory over the little kingdom whose main city sat on an island rock just off shore. Its name means "rock." Because Babylonia was not a naval power, it took the big power of the east thirteen years to subdue the city. This whole passage in chapter 26 is a good illustration of how later editors and copyists added, and sometimes confused, materials. The chapter begins with a date that would place this statement from Ezekiel before the fall of Jerusalem, yet it accuses Tyre of being happy about the wall of Jerusalem being broken and the city laid waste already. Then it launches into the prediction that Tyre will fall as Jerusalem did. But when it gets down to details, the author seems to have knowledge of another sack of Tyre many years later (332 B.C.) by Alexander and the Greek armies.

In the case of both, Babylonia and Greece, the "daughters of the mainland," the suburbs of the island city on the coast were wiped out first. But Alexander took the stones from the buildings of the suburbs and used them to build a causeway about 200 feet wide from the shore to the island. He was then able to use the seigeworks and weapons described in Ezekiel 26 against the walls of the city which he took in seven months. Once into the city, Alexander wiped it out, using the building materials from the buildings and houses there to make the causeway even wider, so that Tyre was now a peninsula instead of an island. Ezekiel put it bluntly, "God will have that rock scraped bare, and it will only be good for laying out fishermen's nets to dry."

His prediction, or the prediction of the later editor who added the description of Alexander's destruction, that "the city would never be rebuilt" was incorrect, however. Tyre stands there today, even after a recent attack from Israel. The *Ezekiel* account says that Tyre is not just going to be conquered; it is going to be so destroyed and cast into the sea that the other islands of the sea are going to mourn its passing. Tyre would be pressed down into the Pit, into Sheol, into the nether regions below the surface of the sea.

The only proper dirge for Tyre would be like a lament for a sunken Titanic, so Ezekiel sings about the Good Ship Tyre, a ship that was considered to be perfect. It was the "state of the art" model of the shipbuilding business. All the planks were of the finest fir, with a great cedar of Lebanon fashioned into the main mast. The oars for the galley were of sturdiest oak, and the planks of the deck were the finest pine, inlaid with ivory. Sails of embroidered linen from Egypt caught the winds and carried her along, while an awning of blue and purple from the Isle of Cyprus protected from the sun. The rowers and pilots, the repair crew and workmen were the finest of the coastal cities of Phoenicia. The whole of the island city of Tyre is a ship where merchants gather from all over the world to barter for merchandise. Protected by walls and towers, manned by mercenaries from many nations whose colorful shields decorated the city-ship's hull, merchants from far-away Spain brought precious metals to exchange for other goods. Traders from Greece, Asia Minor, Syria and Armenia bought and sold slaves, horses, bronze vessels, exchanged wares for ivory and ebony, emeralds, wool and wine, iron and figs and wheat, and all the other goods produced from southern Arabia and east Africa to northern Europe. (The list in chapter 27 is exhaustive and colorful.)

So there you were, the song concludes, sitting there in the heart of the sea filled with all the good things of the world, and there the east wind wrecked you! Your perfect ship, and everything in it, sank on the day of your ruin. All your workmen, and all your suppliers, and all your customers stand on the shore and wail bitterly, but they can do nothing to help you. Now you, the greatest supplier in the world, are sunk beneath the sea with nothing left in your hold. You are gone, forever gone, and there will never be another vessel like you!

Still, chapter 28 brings more of the Tyre story. Perhaps the prophet spent more time denouncing Tyre than all the other small nations put together because the king of Tyre did one thing that was undoubtedly the worst thing anyone could do; he set himself up as God. He sat in his island kingdom thinking he was a god of the sea. He prided himself on his wisdom, and that was O.K. with the prophet. In fact, people had to admit that it took a pretty wise fellow to amass all the commerce and wealth that he had racked up in Tyre. But when he thought he was as wise as God, then God had to act to show him who really is God everywhere, not just in Israel. And God's action involves turning a conqueror loose on the island kingdom.

"Will you still say that you are God in the presence of those who will slay you?" Ezekiel asks. "No, you are just a man, and you will die as a man by the hand of foreigners. So I will sing a little lament for you too."

See *Ezekiel* 28:11-19 for his more beautiful way of putting this final dig from the Lord at the very Human Being king of Tyre who believed his own press reports.

"You were like a perfect diamond on creation
morn,
Dazzling in the starlight as each element was
born,
You the centerpiece for every precious stone,
And gold the perfect setting for yourself alone.
I set a guardian angel to protect your purity;
Your wisdom made you mighty for all the world
to see,
Till greed became your motive, and violence your
way,
And you lost the balanced glory of an earlier day.
So I cast you out, a common stone to be
An example I determined that all the world should
see.

To build your trade you ignored the common
     human worth
And thought that wealth would give you lordship
     of the earth,
But the primeval fires of creation which shape
     everything anew
Turn now to destruction to make an ash of you!''
The End. Amen.

And that was all for Tyre. Now, as to Sidon, just down
the coast, the forecast is not much better. True, the city
won't be thrown into the sea, but disease and sword will
make the streets run red with blood before the Lord's
judgment of Sidon is completed. So all the neighbor
states who were contemptuous of Israel's defeat will now
suffer the same fate. And when a remnant of Israel is
gathered again in the homeland, the Jews will be able
to live secure from threats by their neighbors.

Having pronounced doom on the small nations around
Judah, the prophet now turns, as Jeremiah did, to the
nation on whom Zedekiah's bunch thought they could
rely— Egypt. It was the twelfth day of the tenth month
of the tenth year when he was moved to announce:

"Thus says the Lord God:

" 'Pharaoh, king of Egypt, grandest crocodile in the Nile,
you think you made the great Nile River and that it is your
private stream. I am going to draw you out of there with
hooks, and throw you and the fish that stick to you into
the desert where birds and animals will have you for food.'

(Pharaoh Hophra did bring an army up from Egypt to
try to lift the Babylonian seige of Jerusalem in 588 B.C.
Zedekiah and his assistants thought he would succeed.
The real prophets knew he wouldn't. Perhaps the "fish
that stick to the great croc's scales" were mercenaries,
hired by Pharaoh to join his expedition. Nebuchad-

rezzar's army met him in the desert and defeated the Egyptian forces.)

" 'No longer will Judah have the hope of aid from you. As a strong staff for Judah to lean on, you have turned out to be a flimsy reed which broke, injuring the one who put his trust in you for support. Sooner or later you are going to meet the same destruction that is coming to Judah. Your people will be scattered among the nations, and your land will be desolate for forty years. After forty years, I will gather the remaining Egyptians and let them begin to be a nation again. But Egypt will never again be a powerful nation, ruling over others!' "

Ezekiel's expectation, shared by Jeremiah and others, that Babylon would someday overrun the Egyptian homeland never was fulfilled, but Babylon did break Egypt as a great world power. Succeeding Persian and Greek and Roman empires never allowed it to be a dominant force in world affairs again. Ezekiel's line of reasoning, which he thought the Lord was running through his mind, was interesting. Nebuchadrezzar had worked for years after taking Judah to take the kingdom of Tyre, the fortified island city. Finally he had taken it, but though he had worked his men until "every head was made bald and every shoulder rubbed bare," they never got anything out of Tyre to pay for all the expenses of that campaign of thirteen years. So the ruler of Babylon can plunder Egypt, reimburse his soldiers, and come out with a little profit on the side. After all, he labored pretty hard to help the Lord prove to the king of Tyre that he was no god.

In chapter 30, the prophet again waxes poetical to say that Egypt, plus all her allies from north Africa and the Arabian peninsula, will be slain by the sword of the Lord (again wielded by Babylon's army). The verses through

12 are all more than familiar to us now, and in verses 13 and following the prophet gets down to the main interest of the *Bible* composers. The idols and images of Egypt, gods in competition with the One God of the universe, must be destroyed. As long as the Egyptians, or any other nation, fail to honor the true Creator of all the world they will keep being struck down. One by one their cities are listed, like railroad stops on this track of divine destruction. Their young men will be killed and their women taken captive.

Shortly before the final collapse of Jerusalem, Ezekiel speaks to the people who still hope for rescue by the army of Pharaoh Hophra though the Egyptians were turned back about a year before.

"You are wrong if you think the Pharaoh's broken arm is healed, and that he can come back to beat the Babylonians. It has never healed, and before long the Lord will see that his good arm is broken too. It is the arms of the king of Babylon that will be strengthened by the Lord, and he will wield the sword that scatters the Egyptians as captives among the nations."

Two months later (chapter 31) he had this to direct toward the Pharaoh:

"You know what you are like right now?

"A cedar of Lebanon, a tall one with its head in the clouds and great spreading branches, and with streams flowing around the place it is planted. Towering high above all the other trees of the forest, it has birds forever nesting in its branches while the animals of the forest make a home beneath them. No other cedar or fir could rival its beauty and strength; no tree could begin to match it in the whole garden of God.

"But the loggers are coming, foreigners who will cut down this great tree, causing it to crash and break its branches. There they will leave it, fallen and ruined, and all that lived in its shade and protection will go away. Other great trees have gone this way of destruction, and now it is your turn to join them in the Pit."

Even after the fall of Jerusalem, when many of the survivors still looked to Egypt for refuge, Ezekiel still baited the pro-Egyptian party with a funeral dirge for Pharaoh in 32:1-8.

"You are like a dragon lying in your rivers and muddying them with your feet, and God is going to throw a net over you and haul you out. You will be thrown out into the open field to rot. Birds and beasts will feast on your flesh, and your blood will fill the streambeds. The sun and the moon will be covered in your land and darkness will settle down with your death."

Who is going to be the instrument of the Lord in bagging the great crocodile of the Nile? It is still Nebuchadrezzar. When he and the Babylonians get through with Egypt, the streams that make up the Nile will all run clear because there will be no Egyptian feet to muddy them.

Almost a year before the "dragging the dragon out of the river" speech, Ezekiel had been told by the Lord to "wail over the multitude of Egypt" because they were on their way down to the Pit. That's where the dead go, and that's what they are going to be before long. They will have lots of company there, of course. Assyria, who did so much slaying with the sword will be there, slain by the sword. There also will be the warriors of Elam, along with those who spread terror from Meshech and Tubal. Edom is there. So is Sidon. And when Pharaoh sees them in Sheol he will know that he is in the right company: those who have gone down in shame because of all the terror they caused by their military might.

There seems to be a special place saved for the uncircumcised who are slain by the sword, maybe a little lower level of the Pit than that reserved for regular people who die regular deaths.

Editors of the book of *Ezekiel* placed the "doom" passages first, then slipped in these chapters 25-32 as oracles against other nations, and then finished out the book with passages of hope. Chapter 33 bridges into the hope passages by reviewing an idea that Ezekiel had turned over in his mind in chapter 3. The prophet is to be like a guard in a watchtower, keeping an eye out for an enemy attack. If he sees one coming and blows a trumpet to warn the people who gave him the job of watching, it is up to them to be on guard. If the attackers then come and take them away, it is their own fault. But if the watcher sees the attack coming and does not warn the people, the blame for their conquest is clearly on him.

So the prophet of the Lord must warn sinners of the consequences of their sins. The prophet must appeal to the sinners to change their ways and return to the Lord's way. And if the wicked persons will not repent, they shall die in their sins, but no guilt sticks to the prophet who warned them.

Once again God says, "Let's get one thing straight. I take no pleasure in having anyone turn from the way of Life to the way of death. I want every wicked person to turn back and live. Why will you die, O House of Israel? The goodness of the good person will not save that person from having to take the consequences if he or she turns away from goodness and sins. Likewise, the wickedness of an unrighteous person will not bind him or her to death if that person changes from doing bad to doing good. Obviously the righteous persons will find more life, but if they begin to think that they have it made, and then begin to slip into evil ways, they will discover that their former righteousness won't cover for them now. Obviously the wicked persons will die, but if they stop doing wrong, make amends for whatever wrongs they have done to others, and begin to obey My commandments for life, then they will surely live, not die.''

Chapter 33:21 gives a date that is incorrect, but would be more reasonable if it read the "tenth day of the fifth month of the twelfth year of Jehoiachin's exile.'' It was during the fourth month of that year that the Babylonians breached the wall of Jerusalem, but it took them a while to mop up the defenders and to catch Zedekiah who slipped through the wall and got past Jericho before they nabbed him and his remaining troops. So it was the fifth month before they got back to destroy the temple and the city. It was then that a refugee gets to wherever Ezekiel was with the news, and the prophet's thought was this:

''People keep saying 'Abraham was only one man, but he got possession of this land. Since we are many, we certainly will keep possession of it.' God says that people like you who do not keep the religious laws, who worship idols instead of God, and who shed innocent blood, cannot possibly possess the land. No, in city or town or open country, they will be torn from the land violently. And the land will be left desolate.''

This final catastrophe was proof that the prophet had been right all along.

There had come a time in his preaching career that Ezekiel had been forced to take a hard look at what his preaching was actually accomplishing. Crowds were good at the regular meetings. A lot of people said they "enjoyed the sermon" as they left the gathering place. He and his sermons were the topic of conversation for many a small group around town, and people were saying to each other:

"Hey, if you really want to hear an interesting speaker, come with us to hear our pastor, Ezekiel, this week. You can just tell when you listen to him that he has a word from the Lord."

But "enjoying his sermons" and changing their lives because of them were two different things, Ezekiel had come to realize. He knew that he was popular, but he questioned whether he was effective. And the Lord assured him that he had reason to wonder. They would applaud even when he told them they were headed for destruction. Too bad, but the only way they would finally know that he was truly a prophet, and not just an interesting performer, would be when the destruction finally came. (33:30-33)

Ranching had always been the main occupation of most Hebrew families, and the main contributor to the Hebrew economy. So even city folks knew how to talk about sheep raising. Often preachers alluded to shepherds and sheep, much as they do today, but chapter 34 is an entire sermon on sheep and their caretakers, going into much detail.

"This sermon today," Ezekiel began, "is aimed at those shepherds of our nation who have been busier feeding themselves than the sheep!"

"O boy, this will be a good one," most of the audience thought. "He is going to lay into the government leaders again."

And he did. "Your job is to feed the sheep of Israel, but you are so busy eating lamb chops and making wool clothes for yourselves that you never feed the sheep you are using. You never bother to strengthen the weak ones, take care of the sick ones, or go after the strays when they wander off and get lost. You abuse them instead of caring for them. So they get scattered, and all the wild beasts around attack them at will. Now they are to be found on every high hill and mountain around the country."

"He means that the people who are allowed by the leaders to go to the 'high places' for worshipping idols are lost," one listener whispered to another. "Yes, and pagan cults devour them," the other answered. "I get his point."

"Well, because the shepherds are allowing the sheep of Israel to become a prey for other groups, and because the shepherds have not tended to their business at all, God is going to step in and kick the shepherds out of their jobs. If anybody rescues any of the lost sheep it will have to be the Lord. Fortunately, God is able to do that. Some of the scattered sheep will finally be brought back to the fold. They will find good pasture once again, and good care, because God will be the shepherd who feeds the whole flock with justice. The weak, and crippled, and lost, as well as the healthy and strong, will find a place in the new sheepfold.

"As for the flock now, God is judging the sheep that are gentle and cooperative from the selfish ones who eat wherever they please, not caring if they trample into the mud the food that should be left for others. There are some who not only drink from the stream or pool, but they muddy the water so that others can't get a good drink to quench their thirst. The fat sheep who are doing the pushing and shoving, butting the weak ones aside, are going to be cut out of the flock. A new shepherd from the House of David will be brought in;

the flock will be cared for properly once again.

"The new shepherd will run the wild beasts off the 'high places' and the sheep of Israel will be able to live (and worship) in safety anywhere in the country. The Lord will restore the land to be fruitful and prosperous once more. No longer will Judah be despised by the other nations, but the great come-back which Judah will make will be a sure sign to the world that it is the Lord Who is taking care of the flock."

In the minds of the compilers of the book, part of the good news about some future restoration of Judah's fortunes had to include reprisals on the land of Edom which lay to the south of Judah. The Edomites came into the part of Judah adjacent to them after the Babylonians had laid waste to much of it. They looted what was left and, according to chapter 35, had designs on taking over the two countries (Judah and Israel). This prophecy against Mount Seir (a name used here for all the hill country of Edom) says that the Lord will repay them in kind. Their people will be killed, and their country laid waste, never to be a force to be reckoned with again.

It is true that Edom, like Judah, was through the next centuries to be overrun by foreign empires, but it isn't true that Edom was to be ground down so much that it could never influence Judah again. On the contrary, Edomite possessions in southern Judah continued to grow until a son of Edom ruled all of Palestine with the title of Herod the Great.

"So the mountains of Edom are going to suffer the same kind of devastation that the mountains of Israel have suffered," Ezekiel adds in chapter 36.

The New Jerusalem

He starts off with a sentence that would give anyone who tries to diagram it fits. In the Revised Standard Version of the *Bible* it takes five verses to get to the period. If he had been a lawyer instead of a preacher, the sentence would have read like this:

"WHEREAS the enemy said 'Aha! We have these mountains for our possession,' and

"WHEREAS they made you desolate, so that you became the subject of malicious gossip on all sides from people who now claim you, and

"WHEREAS the Lord has something to say to you mountains and hills, valleys and ravines, desolate wastes and ruined cities,

"NOW THEREFORE, BE IT RESOLVED, that the Lord take care of Edom and the other nations that took advantage of you, and that they themselves will suffer reproach.

"There is hope. This ruined country of Israel will become fruitful again. Farms and ranches will be restored as they were, and towns and cities will be rebuilt. There will be more people, and more prosperity than this land has ever known before.

"It was the fault of our own people of Israel that all this wrath came on us in the first place. God allowed us to be scattered among the nations, and people there have made so much fun of us saying 'These were the Lord's people, but look what happened to them,' that the Lord will bring us back for the sake of the Lord's own reputation. But we will have to clean up our act. The idols have to go, and we have to be baptized all over again into God's way.

"The Lord will give us a new heart, a new spirit. God's own Spirit will live in us to teach us how to walk in the Way of Life. Once again the Promised Land will be ours because once again the covenant with God will be ours. And when we see how good and fruitful life with the Lord can be, we will be ashamed that we ever left it in the first place. It won't be because of any good in us that God will do all this; it will be only to show what grace and mercy the Lord can share. When the land becomes a veritable Garden of Eden, and the remnant of Israel has increased again to a great populous nation, all the world will see and worship the Lord. That's the point of it all."

That sounds good now as we read it, but it might have sounded like a hollow wish in the actual situation when the population was almost wiped out. It took someone with the peculiar insight of the prophet who dreamed in big-screen, technicolor visions to penetrate the dark present to see a different future. One of the most famous Ezekiel visions comes in chapter 37.

"The Lord set me down in the middle of a valley, and it was filled with dry bones. It was death valley plus, dry as could be, and the bones lying all around. There were a lot of them too. And the Spirit asked me: 'Do you think these bones can live?'

"I said, 'I don't know, Lord. Only You know that.'

" 'Well, speak to them. Preach to them and say to these dry bones 'Now, hear the word of the Lord. God is going to put muscles and flesh and skin on you again, and God is going to breathe the breath of life in you again. You will live again and know that the Lord is God.' "

So Ezekiel made that speech to the dry bones in the valley, and he began to hear a strange sound while he was talking. It was the sound of dry bones rattling together. One by one the bones put themselves together in the right order, and bodies began shaping up around them. There they were, instead of dry bones, lifeless bodies whole and complete lying there!

"We have to have some breath in them, son of man," the Lord said. "Call for breath to come out of the four winds, so these bodies can live."

Ezekiel obeyed. "Breath of life, come back into these bodies," he called out; "the Lord commands it!" And there was a stirring of the breeze, and the bodies came to life. Here and there people started getting to their feet until there was a whole valley full of people standing around him.

"You know who these people are?" the Lord inquired. "These people are from the House of Israel. They are the people who are so beaten and discouraged right now that they are saying to themselves, 'we are dead; our bones are dried up; we've had it!' I want you to preach to them and encourage them. Tell them not to give up because I will bring them back to the land of Israel, like bringing the dead back from their graves. I will put My Spirit within you and you will live to know that I am the Lord Who does all this!"

Why has that been one of H.B.'s favorite dreams across the centuries? Is it because every H.B. sooner or later gets that dry-bone feeling, "This is the end; I can't go on; it's hopeless?" If any new life is to come, it has to be from outside him/herself. It has to be a new breath of life from the Creator of Life. And, impossible as it seems, it happens. H.B. stands up again to carry on.

In verse 15 the dry bones give way to sticks, two sticks in the prophet's hand. The Lord says to Ezekiel, "write

'Judah' on one of them, and 'Israel' on the other."

"All right, and then what am I going to do with them?" Ezekiel wondered.

"Hold them tightly together in one fist, and when people ask you 'what are you doing?' tell them 'the Lord is going to make the two sticks of Israel into one again.' God is going to bring some of the exiled people of Israel back, also some of the exiled people of Judah back. Together they will form one nation again. They will be clean of idols, and noble of character, once more the People of God. Their one ruler will be the house of David, and their one holy place will be the temple which will be restored in their midst."

Chapter 38 takes the picture farther into the future. Out of *Genesis*, chapter 10, a number of names are pulled. They represent all kinds of lands and people on the outskirts of the world as the Jews knew it. At some undisclosed time in the future, long after Israel has been resettled, a ruler called Gog (nobody knows exactly which historical ruler may have been the inspiration for this mythical character) will be practically forced by the Lord to form a great alliance of nations who will come to attack Israel. The sole purpose of their attack is to set up the occasion where the Lord can show that Israel needs no other protection than the Lord. God is setting them up for the kill, which will show all the nations of the world Who is God around here. But on the way, Gog gets greedy. Seeing all the towns and open country of Israel lying unprotected by military defense, he wants to plunder the easy pickings. No armed towers, no solid gates, no walls to break down; these people who have been gathered from the dispersion will be ripe for the taking. This greed now makes Gog and his allies the bad guys (not God Who brought them here by a hook in the nose), so God must respond to their challenge to the Chosen People. And it will be a comprehensive and violent response.

The great armies of Gog are like a cloud covering the earth, but no army will meet them from Israel. Only the wrath of the Lord of Israel will fight against them. Earthquakes will shake the earth apart. Hills and walls will fall on the aggressors. Torrential rains and hailstones plus fire and brimstone will pour down on them from the skies, while plagues and fighting among themselves wipe them out on the ground.

Then, the writers thought, everyone would be obliged to acknowledge the Lord of Israel as the God of all the earth. Other H.B.s, desiring to see the same goal achieved, felt that God would take a little different tack. God's best representatives might show so much love and creativity that people everywhere would want to live the kind of life which centered around the worship of that kind of God. Twenty-five hundred years later, God's people are still divided on the same issue. When God finally does establish the "Kingdom of God" on earth, will it be done with a sword after luring the forces of the world into a final show-down massacre? Or will it be achieved through the same methods of love that Jesus used, bearing a cross instead of a sword?

In chapter 39, the same story of the Lord bringing Gog, etc. into a final showdown is told in a little different way. God is pictured as pushing the attackers toward Israel, then knocking the weapons right out of their hands when they get there. Their armies will be left dead in the fields as prey for wild birds and animals. The people of Israel will only have to clean up the fields, because dead human bodies make the land ceremonially unclean. But that in itself will be quite a job. They will collect so many bows, arrows, and wooden spears that they won't have to cut firewood for seven years. They will haul the remains of the soldiers to a valley east of the Dead Sea, the place where Gog himself will be buried too. It will take seven months just to haul the dead to the valley. People will find bodies everywhere, and will report their find to the hauling squads. If anyone sees a bone, or any human remain, in a field or along a roadway, he or she will stick up a sign by it so the special burying forces can take it away. Meanwhile the birds and wild animals will have a special feast on the carcasses of the once-mighty army of Gog and his compatriots.

The object of all this carnage? The same as in every one of these oracles about the days of Judah's restoration—God will be recognized world-wide as God. First the Lord's glory was seen in the punishment of Israel after Israel went astray. Finally, it will be seen in the reestablishment of Israel and the crushing of all her enemies.

About thirteen years after the fall of Jerusalem, Ezekiel was still seeing and hearing messages from the Lord, and still passing them on to the people. Begin reading chapter 40 and ask him, "What is this one about, son of man?"

"Let me tell you. I pictured myself as on the top of a mountain, looking at a model of a city exactly like the temple area was. There was a man there, bronze and brilliant in appearance, with a flax string and a measuring stick in his hand. He was standing by the gate nearest me.

" 'I want you to watch and listen carefully, because you are supposed to report everything I show you to the people of Israel.' That's what he told me. So I noticed there was a wall all around the outside of the temple area. The measuring stick in his hand was a little over 10 feet long, so when he measured the thickness of the wall I saw that it was ten feet thick. It was also 10 feet high." Later they would measure the length of the wall as well. The wall extended around an area that was perfectly square and almost 900 feet on each side. Ezekiel wasn't thinking in terms of American football fields, but if he had he would have noted that this area would cover about 18 of them. Much of the over 800,000 square feet was an outdoor courtyard, paved with brick and tile. Around three sides of the outer edge of the open area, up against the inside of the 10-foot-thick wall, were thirty very large rooms where lay persons could spend the night dormitory-style or have group meals served there by the Levite cooks who worked out of the kitchens which were built into each corner of the wall. In the center of each wall on the north, east, and south walls were gates, flanked by rooms where security guards were stationed. Once past the guard houses, a person entered the outer court and was looking at the temple itself which stood on a raised stone platform 10 feet higher than the level of an inner courtyard which was itself eight steps higher than the outer court. All together it was larger than one of the football field areas. The back end of the building complex was placed against the western wall, so there was no gateway into the courtyard from that side.

To get up to the temple area, a pilgrim had to mount eight steps up through another series of guard stations and gates exactly like the outer gates and rooms. Again they were placed on the north, east, and south sides of the inner court. In the center of that court stood an enormous altar, built like a stepped pyramid, flat on top. The top was about 20 feet square, and the base of it measured about 30 feet on each side. Sticking up from each corner of the top altar-hearth surface were four "horns" or points, one on each corner. From base to top it rose over 20 feet, and that point would be the highest point on which people could stand in the whole layout of the city. It tied earth and heaven together for the Jewish worshippers, a place where life was sacrificed to praise the Giver of all life. Some of those Jewish worshippers questioned whether the Creator preferred having Human

Beings sacrificing other animal beings for Human Being sins and/or praise.

"Perhaps," some of them said, "God would rather have H.B. offer his/her own life, not in dying but in living, as the Creator means for human life to be lived. Sacrificing a goat or lamb may not mean that the self-centeredness of the human's inner being is being sacrificed at all. And if it isn't, then God is still not recognized or worshipped as God by that unsurrendered person. Besides, it doesn't seem fair to treat other animals that way."

But, whatever the theological thought, the altar was there in Ezekiel's vision. In that inner court were also the cutting tables, the wash basins, and all the paraphernalia necessary for an extremely large butchery and "sacrifice" operation. Continuing from the inner court up steps on the east side you would rise to the vestibule of the temple itself. Past the large pillars that stood by the entrance, you entered the vestibule, then the nave, and past that the inner place or most holy place. There is no ark of the covenant, and no great cherubim. The only furnishing mentioned is an altar made of wood almost 4 feet square, probably the table where the Bread of the Presence (or show bread) was kept. All the sanctuary is paneled with wood which was decorated with palm trees and cherubs.

There were other rooms associated with the operation of the temple, plus all the housing and living areas necessary for the many priests who worked there. If you have plenty of time and patience, you can go ahead and follow Ezekiel's Spirit Guide with his 10-foot-long measuring stick while he calls out each detail of each part of the construction. But suffice it to say that it was to be a very imposing center for Jewish celebrations of worship. And all of it was just a stage setting for the real drama which begins in chapter 43.

Ezekiel is standing by the east gate when he saw the glory of God, coming like sunlight in the morning, to enter the temple that was prepared for that Presence. Once again the prophet falls on his face, and once again the Spirit lifts him up to see the glory of God filling the whole temple. And he hears a Voice that says "This is where I am going to stay now. The people of Israel are not going to profane My Name again with worship of idols and false gods, nor with burying their kings here. The graveyards are going to be separated from this holy area. I plan to stay here forever.

"You go tell the people now," the Voice continues, "that this is the new 'Law of the Temple', that all the land around the temple on this hilltop is to be considered holy."

So the temple is ready. Now let's get the people ready. It will take seven days of the proper ritual connected with sacrifices at the new altar. Verses 18-27 of chapter 43 tell which animals are to be sacrificed on which days and why and how. If it is done correctly, then the Lord will be open for business, accepting the worshippers from the eighth day on.

Since God had entered the east entrance, it ought to be kept shut from now on. It would be O.K. for a king to sit there and share a meal in spirit with the Lord, but in the future everybody else could use the north and south entrances only.

"Another thing, Ezekiel," the Spirit added, "tell the people of Israel that they are not to let any foreigners in this inner temple area. You let them in before, and they caused you to adulterate your pure worship. They would do it again.

"As for the Levites who allowed sacrifices to other idols, they will get to do the servant jobs around here, preparing the animals for sacrifice, serving the people meals, and making up the security forces as well as the custodial corps.

But they will not get to come near the sacred things, or do any of the tasks assigned to the priests. This will be their punishment for helping to lead the people of Israel astray. The sons of Zadok kept themselves clean of all that harlotry before the old temple was destroyed. Only they may present offerings to Me, take care of the holy area and the altar table. They are to wear all-linen outfits, no wool, and nothing to make them sweat. When they go outside the inner court and the sanctuary, they can wear regular clothes, but inside they have to have their priest clothes on.

"You see, we have to keep the holy things separated from the common or secular world. We don't want them spreading holiness around outside the temple area." (44:19) (Holiness is catching, just as sickness is. One would think that a whole epidemic of holiness, or wholeness, would be a good thing for a community. I'm sure Ezekiel thought so too, but knew instinctively that the way to spread it is not by allowing "holy" garments to be touched by those who weren't in on the sacrificing it takes to make them holy.)

In the new temple, things were going to be pretty strict on the priests. Following the instructions about temple garments, the list continues:

. . . no shaved heads, no long hair, just neatly trimmed.

. . . no drinking wine before entering the inner court for duty.

. . . no marrying a widow or divorced woman, except the widow of another priest.

. . . teach the people to distinguish between clean and unclean.

. . . act as judges when controversy arises.

. . . keep all the feasts, and all the sabbath days.

. . . keep away from all dead persons, except for immediate family members.

. . . remember that it takes seven days of waiting after touching a dead body before the sin offering can be made that will assure that you are clean again.

. . . own no property, have no inheritance. The food offerings at the temple will take care of all needs. Those first offerings of fruit, grain, and meat are mighty nice.

. . . never eat anything that died by itself, or was torn apart.

Chapter 45:1-8 adds that the priests and Levites, who are supposed to never again own any land of their own, need to have a space around the temple reserved for their families to live. Chapter 48 gives even more details. They get an area about eight miles square; the priests get a three-mile-wide strip of it, and the Levites get a similar strip. The third, smaller strip, is reserved for the capital city itself. Somewhere, probably at the center of the priest's section, is the temple area. Also the king's government is given an area separated from the rest of the city.

Mention of this "capital area," reminds the prophet to warn the government leaders that their area is all they get; they are not to evict poor people from their land anywhere else, nor levy any more taxes than are necessary to support the temple. And they are to give themselves to seeing that justice is done, and the civil peace is kept. (45:9)

The I.R.S. (Israeli Revenue Service) should keep honest books, and weigh out the taxes with honest scales. No mention is made of interest for back taxes. They were to make sure that an ephah and a bath measured the same, both measuring one tenth of a homer. A "bath" was a liquid measurement of several gallons, and an "ephah" was a dry measure of less than two bushels. Measurements in the marketplaces were not all the same. At the temple they were to be a standard measurement to make sure the Lord (represented by the temple officials) got a correct share.

They weighed out the money too, just to make sure each silver dollar weighed an ounce. When you brought a shekel in, it had better be a full-weight shekel.

Taxes didn't take such a big bite in Ezekiel's plan as they did in practice later on. You had only to put in one bushel of grain out of every sixty you produced, and only one gallon of oil out of every hundred gallons. One sheep for every two hundred you owned took care of the tax on livestock. The king's I.R.S. collected the taxes and furnished the temple what the priests needed for the operations there.

In case any sin slipped by unnoticed in the temple, the temple itself had to be "cleansed" twice a year, on New Year's Day then again on the first day of the seventh month (not the seventh day of the first month as some translations put it). Sprinkling or painting blood of a young bull here and there was their idea of cleansing. The passover began on the fourteenth day of the first month, with instruction given for that observance in the last five verses of chapter 45.

There should be a sign on the east gate of the inner court which reads:

"This gate is shut, except on the sabbath. (New moon days are exceptions.)"

When you entered one gate (north or south) you had to go out the other. It was "straight ahead and no turning back" when you came to worship at the temple. That might be a good way for any of us to approach the worship of the God who is ever creating anew.

Chapter 46 is full of details about what to sacrifice when. You may not feel that you need to memorize them. The last part of that chapter reports Ezekiel's tour of the kitchen areas of the temple compound. And the questions begin to creep into your mind as you read: What if God were a vegetarian? Or what if the Hebrew religion had been developed in an area where animals were scarce? Maybe as people of India did, they would have let "sacred cows" walk around among them instead of butchering them in honor of God.

The temple will be a source of life renewal, even for the desert to the east. Flowing out from under the temple will be a miraculous stream which Ezekiel said in effect "you have to see it to believe!" The farther it goes the deeper it gets, even though no other tributaries flow into it. Trees grow along its banks, and when it flows into the Dead Sea, it makes the waters fresh (all except some marshes where the salt water will still furnish salt which was a necessary commodity.) Fishing so good that fishermen will stand shoulder to shoulder on the shore with everybody catching all they want—that is a dream!

It brings us back almost to the Garden of Eden days. And that is what we are aiming for, Ezekiel would have admitted. Now, let's get the old territory divided out among the tribes again, dividing it into 12 strips which run east and west across country from the Mediterranean Sea to the Jordan River, and from Syria on the north to Egypt on the south. But this is not to be an armed conquest of the Promised Land all over again. Aliens, non-Jews who live in the area, are to be given equal rights with the tribe that possess it.

A resettlement of Israel under Ezekiel's conditions would have had a much better chance of producing a stable situation for H.B.'s life in the Middle East than the original settlement under Joshua's plan. Of course, it was just a dream, this bringing back of the "lost tribes" of Israel, unless you include all the rest of us H.B.s in this vision of a world that puts God at the center of all life, as the temple is the center measuring point for all geography. Then wherever we live, and whoever we are, we live in the holy ground area where all life becomes sacred, and all people brothers and sisters in the family of God.

DANIEL

Dream World

"Some of those captives are attractive and intelligent," Nebuchadrezzar, king of great Babylon, said one day. "They could be taught our language and customs, and they would make excellent servants here. Pick some of their leading young men and bring them into the palace. Give them a three-year course of training, and let's see what they can achieve."

Ashpenaz, the chief eunuch, rounded them up. For three years they were treated to the king's table and all that went with life in the richest palace of the world. And when their training period was over, the king wanted to check them out. Four young men from the tribe of Judah were among those selected to appear before the monarch: Daniel, Hananiah, Mishael, and Azariah.

The first thing the king did was to give them Babylonian names. If he were going to make good Babylonians out of them, that was a good place to start. Belteshazzar was the new name he tagged onto Daniel. Hananiah he called Shadrach; Mishael he named Meshach; and Abednego was the new name for Azariah.

Daniel was a teetotaler when it came to drink, and also kept himself on a rigorous diet. The kind of eating and drinking which went along with the royal household was more than he could indulge with a good conscience. Fortunately, the chief eunuch was a reasonable man. He didn't want to force Daniel and his three friends to break their religious vows, but he did have to consider the consequences to himself if these four turned out weaker and poorer in appearance than the other young men who were being fattened at the king's table.

"The king put me in charge of building you up," the eunuch said, "and he will have my head if he sees you are in poorer condition than the others."

"Well, would you go for a little test then?" Daniel asked him. "Give us vegetables to eat and water to drink for ten days. Then check our appearance against the young men who are eating the rich food and drinking wine."

"All right, ten days. I'll give you that much," the eunuch agreed.

The story doesn't note that Daniel and his friends probably worked out every day in the royal gym. But after the ten-day period the chief eunuch observed that the boys from Judah were healthier in appearance than the rich-food-and-wine ones. So, much to the dismay of the others, no doubt, he ordered all the young men to be put on the vegetarian diet with only water to drink!

Likewise, in all their training, the Hebrew Four excelled. It also developed during this three-year period that Daniel not only was smart, he could interpret dreams. (Another ancestor of his, named Joseph, had risen from slavery in a bygone empire to become a favorite of the king's realm by interpreting deams. One thing about it: when a good idea works once, the Lord remembers it for use again.)

The final examination was no contest at all; the four from Judah stood head and shoulders above the rest in all the subjects in the Babylonian palace curriculum.

"These are the ones I want for my advisers,"

Nebuchadrezzar decided. And Daniel filled the role of adviser to the king all the rest of the exile period.

Now, before we begin the chapter 2 story, the first of the series found in the first six chapters, let's pause to take a look at when and why the book was put together in the first place.

The stories had come down for four centuries. Back in the time when the people of Judah had lived as exiles in Babylonia and other lands of that great empire which had destroyed Jerusalem, true worshippers of the Lord God of Israel had been pressured mightily to give up their religion. Some of them did, but others held fast to their faith, even when tortured and killed. One of the faithful was this good man named Daniel. And the stories about Daniel and some of his staunch friends were told and retold in the Aramaic language which had become the common language of the Jews in exile, and which continued through New Testament times.

Sometime during the three-year period of Jewish revolt following the terrible desecration of the Jewish temple on Dec. 6, 167 B.C., a writer pulls these stories together to encourage the Jews of his day not to give up in their flight against the king, Antiochus IV Epiphanes of Syria and Palestine, who had built an altar to the Greek god Zeus on the altar of God in the temple.

"If Daniel and his companions could hold true in the days of Babylon, we can do it in our time of trial," the author of *Daniel* urged his people as they rebelled against the heirs to the Middle Eastern part of the great Alexander's Empire. The first six chapters of his book tell the stories of Daniel who lived up to his name which means "God is Judge." He was busy passing on God's judgment to Nebuchadrezzar, king of Babylon, in the years just after he had taken captive many Jews along with their king.

He had looted the temple and taken the golden vessels to put into his own temple. He had also looted many other nations, so it might have been an uneasy conscience that caused him to have a dream one night that troubled him greatly. Here's where we pick up the story.

"I want them all here," the king ordered the next morning, "the magicians, the sorcerers, the enchanters, the astrologers. I want to know the meaning of this dream."

"No problem, your majesty," they said after they gathered before him. "Just tell us the dream and we will give you the interpretation of it."

"No. You are supposed to be so smart. You tell me what the dream was, and then interpret it!"

They looked at each other in dismay. Dismay which turned to great distress, when he added, "If you don't, I am going to have you torn limb from limb, and I'll destroy your homes as well."

"Maybe you misunderstood, your majesty, you have to tell us the dream first before we can interpret it for you."

"No, you misunderstood," the king came back. "You tell me the dream, and then I'll know that you can interpret it. Otherwise you will just agree on some answer and come back with it. So quit stalling."

"You're asking the impossible, your majesty. There isn't a person on earth who can do what you want. No king has ever asked that of us before. It would take a god to answer your request!" That was the only response they could make as they were being led away to the holding cells of the prison.

The king's order included all the "wise men" who were supposed to advise him, so Daniel and his friends were rounded up with the rest of them. That's when Daniel struck up a conversation with Arioch, the captain of the king's guard who was responsible for carrying out the king's order for the executions.

"Doesn't the king's order seem a little severe to you?" Daniel asked. "What's the king's problem?"

The captain told Daniel the whole story, so Daniel asked him for permission to make an appointment with the king to interpret the dream. Arioch said he would do it, knowing that the king really wanted to get the interpretation more than he wanted to kill all his advisers. While he was gone to make the appointment, Daniel met with his three friends and asked them to start praying with him for a vision from the Lord that would clear things up. That night the answer came, and Daniel's prayer of petition turned to a prayer of thanksgiving:

"Blessed be the name of God forever. O Lord, You arrange the seasons; You set up and remove kings; You know what is in the darkness; and now I give You thanks for showing me the answer to the king's problem!"

Arioch hurried Daniel into the king's presence the next morning.

"Here's the man I told you about!"

"Oh, yes, Daniel, the one I named Belteshazzar! You say you can tell me what I dreamed, and then interpret it for me? None of the wise men and magicians around my court can do it."

"Well," Daniel answered politely, "this isn't something people can know, but the God of the heavens knows. This God has been giving you a look in your dream at what is coming in the future. You saw in your dream a large image, very bright and very frightening, didn't you?"

Nebuchadrezzar nodded, now leaning forward with anticipation.

"The head of the image was gold; its chest and arms were silver, and the lower part of its body and thighs were bronze. The legs were iron, and the feet were part iron and part clay. While you were looking at it, a stone came into the picture and struck the image on the feet and shattered them. Then all the rest of the image began to crumble into pieces, so fine that the wind blew them all away like the chaff of wheat from the threshing floor. Not a trace of them could be found, but the stone stayed there. And it started to grow until it became a great mountain that filled the whole earth. That was it, wasn't it?''

Dumfounded, the king nodded again.

''Now, let's tell the king the interpretation. You are the king to whom God has given all the might and glory of this empire. You rule over all; you are the head of gold.''

So far, so good, the king was thinking.

''But after you,'' Daniel continued, ''another kingdom, inferior to yours, will rise, and after that still another— the silver and the bronze. Then there shall be a fourth kingdom, strong as iron, because iron can crush all the others. But, as you saw, the feet are partly of iron and partly of clay, symbolizing a divided kingdom. The iron and clay will mix together in marriage, but they won't hold because iron and clay don't mix. Finally, in those days, the God of heaven will set up a kingdom which will never be destroyed. Just like that stone, it will break to pieces completely everything that has gone before it. This is the dream, and this is the interpretation of it, sent to you through me by the great God of heaven.''

He had never done it to another man before, but King Nebuchadrezzar prostrated himself before Daniel, as if before the God Who had sent the interpretation.

''Your God must be the God of Gods and Lord of kings!'' he said to Daniel. ''And you are going to be my Number One man in this empire.'' (Why not? It happened to Joseph the same way.)

The first thing Daniel did was to get the king to appoint

the three friends as business managers for the chief province of Babylon. Daniel himself stayed in court as the king's right-hand man.

Readers of *Daniel* knew that the three kingdoms to succeed Babylon's were the Medes, the Persians, and the iron empire of Alexander the Great. After Alexander's death, the empire was split between four of his generals. The iron and clay didn't hold together, and by the time of this writing, Judah was under the heel of the Seleucid dynasty of Syria. No human hand would cut it, but a great stone from God would soon come to break the iron-clay foot to pieces, and God's own rule would be set up.

The second story, told in chapter 3, shows that the king's outburst of praise for Daniel's God was soon forgotten by the king himself. Like Antiochus Epiphanes setting the image of Zeus on the sacred altar of the Jewish temple in the writer's time, Nebuchadrezzar in the old days set up an image to be worshipped. It was a big one, ninety feet high, erected in a level plain where thousands could gather around it. Every officer of every province was ordered to be there for the dedication ceremony. A band that included every kind of musical instrument they knew was ready to play the empire anthem. And the order was made clear:

"When you hear the anthem played, don't stand with your hat off; prostrate yourself on the ground and worship this image as God!"

On the downbeat, the music began, and all the officials hastened to do as they had been ordered. All except Shadrach, Meshach and Abednego (no mention is made of Daniel in this story). Of course, there were tattle-tales. People who were jealous of the favored positions of the three Jews rushed to report.

"The three men you appointed to head up the province of Babylon disobeyed you," they told the king. "They are not worshipping your god; they are willfully disobeying your order."

"Bring them here," the furious king bellowed.

"Shadrach, Meshach, Abednego, is it true that you disobeyed my own order to worship the god I set up? Now, let's try it once again. I'm going to have the music start again, and let's see you fall down and worship. Because if you don't, you are going to be thrown into a fiery furnace. Then we will see what god can deliver you."

Now the three gave the answer the writer hopes the Jews of his day will give to those who would force them to worship the Greek god Antiochus was foisting upon them.

"We don't even have to answer you. If our God wants to do it, we will be saved even from the fiery furnace. But, even if not, we still will not serve your gods or worship this golden image you have set up."

The dark look on Nebuchadrezzar's face forecast his decree.

"Make that furnace seven times hotter than usual, and throw them in."

Dressed up completely in all their clothes, even hats, the three were dropped through the flue on top of the kiln. So hot were the flames and gases that came out of the furnace that the men who thrust the intended victims in were scorched themselves.

(Here the Greek version of the Jewish Bible, followed by the Roman Catholic versions, add the "Prayer of Azariah", and the "Song of the Three Young Men." Protestant versions put these passages in the Apocrypha, and do not include them in this text.)

Apparently the king stooped over to look into the furnace a little later, because the *Bible* story says "he rose up in haste," and said to his counselors, "Didn't we just throw three men in that furnace?"

"Yes, three of them," they agreed.

"Then why do I see four? They are all walking around in the middle of the furnace and they are not hurt at all. That fourth one looks like a god!"

Then Nebuchadrezzar ordered the big door of the furnace to be opened.

"Shadrach, Meshach, Abednego, come on out of there this instant!"

And they did. They stepped out of that red-hot furnace without a hair on their heads singed, and without a bit of their clothing burned. In fact, they didn't even smell like they had been near a fire. Once again, as after the Daniel interpretation of his dream, the king praises the God of Israel.

"Anybody who ever says a word against the God of Shadrach, Meshach, and Abednego will be killed. There isn't any other god that is able to deliver in this way!"

As for the three young men, they got their jobs back with a bonus, and larger-lettered names on their doors! (Their message: God can save from fiery furnaces today those who will not worship the graven image of Antiochus.)

The story in chapter 4 begins in the form of a letter from the king to all his subjects:

"I feel compelled to write to tell you about the miraculous things the Most High God has done for me lately. Not long ago, I felt I was getting along nicely, with no worries, when I had a dream that made me afraid. I called in all the wise men who were supposed to be able to interpret dreams, but not one of them could make any sense of it. Finally, I called in Daniel (I call him Belteshazzar because he has the spirit of gods in him), and told him my dream:

"I saw a tree in the middle of the field, greater than any other tree. It reached to heaven, and it could be seen from anywhere in the world. It had wonderful foliage and enough fruit for anyone. Birds and animals found shelter in and under it. Then a herald dropped down from heaven and called out, 'Chop this tree down and cut off its branches; strip off the leaves and scatter the fruit. But leave the stump, circled by a band of iron and bronze, out in the grassy field. (Here the announcement of the heavenly herald changes, but dreams include abrupt switches at times.) Let him be wet with rain and dew; let him live with beasts in the field; let his mind be changed from human to that of an animal, and let seven times pass over him!'

"Now, Daniel, what does that mean? I asked him. Daniel was visibly shaken, but after a while I told him 'Don't be afraid to tell me what you are thinking.'

" 'My Lord,' he said, 'the interpretation of this dream ought to be for those who hate you, for your enemies! The tree is you who now dominate the whole earth. But the word from heaven is that you are to be driven from among people and you shall live among the animals of the field, eating grass like an ox, out in the rain and weather for seven years until you know that the real ruler of all kingdoms is the Most High God. The stump is left in the field, because your kingdom will be waiting for you when you come to realize that God alone rules. The only advice I can give to you now is that you stop your sinning, and show mercy to the people who are now being oppressed by your government. That will stave off this judgment that will come on you otherwise.'

"A year later I was walking on the roof of the palace in Babylon saying to myself, 'Isn't this a great palace and a great empire which I have built with my own power for my own glory?' and it happened. The voice came from heaven and said, 'Nebuchadnezzar, this is it. Today you will go to the field to eat grass like an animal. For seven years you will stay there until you know that the power always belongs to the Most High God, not any human being!'

"You should have seen me. For seven years my hair grew while I was like an animal; my nails even got to be like bird claws. Then my reason returned, and I began to praise God in heaven. I took over this kingdom again. Now the empire is greater than ever before, but I, Nebuchadrezzar, am careful to give all the praise and honor to the King of Heaven."

(If the great King Nebuchadrezzar was driven to acknowledgement of the Lord as the only God, the writer was saying, then modern-day kings and rulers can be convinced as well. They may act like beasts for a while, but sooner or later they will come around. Look for your letter from Antiochus anytime; meanwhile, stand fast in the faith yourself.)

The short story in chapter 5 tells of a great feast given by a descendant of Nebuchadrezzar. His name was Belshazzar and he got drunk in front of thousands of his government officials from all over the empire. Thinking he was funny, he committed a sacreligious act that the Lord did not think was funny at all. In the writer's day, Antiochus was profaning the sacred temple just as Belshazzar profaned the sacred drinking cups Nebuchadrezzar had taken from the temple. For Belshazzar had the Jewish sacred vessels brought in so that he and his party could drink out of them. They even toasted their idols with the Lord's own cups.

It was then that it happened. A hand appeared in the air and began to write on the white plastered wall opposite the king's seat. In the glow of the lampstand nearest it, the drunken king saw the letters forming. People looking at him thought he had seen a ghost. He turned pale and began to shake with fright as he tried to look away, then looked back at the wall. Suddenly it was quiet, with stillness broken only by the quavering voice of the king:

"Bring in the magicians and astrologers and priests."

They came on the double.

"Whoever reads this writing on that wall, and tells me what it means, will be a rich man. I'll make him Number Three in the kingdom." But nobody could claim the reward, because nobody could decipher the message seen by the plastered king on the plaster wall. It was the queen who was still clear headed enough to remind him that there was yet hope for a reading.

"Why don't you call Daniel, the old man who was made chief of all his staff of wise men by Nebuchadrezzar? He never missed on interpreting dreams, and I'll bet he can read and interpret this mysterious writing for you."

So they sent for Daniel, and by the time he arrived the king and the party had sobered up considerably.

"I've heard a lot about you, Daniel," the king began. "They tell me that the spirit of the gods is in you, that you can give interpretations and solve problems better than anyone around. All these fancy wise men of ours have tried to interpret this writing you see on that wall, but none of them could even begin to decipher it. If you can do it, I'll make you a wealthy man, and place you as third-in-command in all the empire."

"Thanks for the offer, but you can keep the gifts and rewards for yourself, or for anybody else. However, I will read the writing and tell you what it means. But first let me remind you that it was the Most High God who gave this empire to Nebuchadrezzar. That king had the power of life and death over all the people of the world, but when he grew proud and haughty because of that power, God took the throne and the glory away from him. He was forced to live like an animal in the field until his spirit was broken and he acknowledged that God alone has the power to make and break all rulers.

"I know you know all this. Still you have decided not to humble yourself before God. You even desecrated the holy vessels of God's temple in Israel by using them for common drinking cups. Even more, you used them for toasts to gods of wood and stone and metal instead of worshipping the One God in Whose hand is your very life itself!

It was God Who sent the hand that wrote this message on your wall: MENE, MENE, TEKEL, PARSIN. The words mean 'numbered, weighed, divided.' God has numbered the days of your kingdom and will bring it to an end. You have been weighed in the balances and found wanting. Your kingdom is divided and given to the Medes and Persians."

Isaiah, Jeremiah, Ezekiel and the other true prophets of old would have been proud of Daniel. He stood before the mightiest ruler of the world and told it like it was. The story doesn't say that Belshazzar was overly concerned. Maybe he thought it would be a good joke on the bringer of such a message to appoint him, against his wishes, as Third Ruler of the Kingdom. Because that night he would have no more kingdom to rule.

Verse 30 says that Belshazzar was killed that very night, and the king of the Medes, Darius I, took over the empire of Babylon.

Darius changed the way the empire was governed, chapter 6 says. Over each of 120 provinces he appointed a governor, and then he divided all the provinces into three administrative areas. Each had a president, and Daniel was one of the three. Of course, it wasn't long before the king could see that Daniel was by far the most able of them all. The word was out that the king planned to make Daniel his civil ruler of all the empire.

The other presidents, and some of the governors, tried

in vain to find something against Daniel that they could use to discredit him with the king. But, finding nothing but good, they had to try a different tack.

"Maybe we can nail him because of his religion," they agreed. And they got up a plan that would cause Daniel's religious faith to discredit him before the king. A committee of them went to the king with this request.

"All of us are agreed that it would be a good thing for the kingdom if you were to issue a decree that everyone has to address prayers only to you for thirty days, not to any other god or person. Punishment for not complying with the law would be that the offender will be thrown into a den of lions. Sign it 'According to the law of the Medes and Persians' so that nobody can ever change it."

Darius was vain enough to sign it.

Now Daniel could see this handwriting on the wall for him. He went into the upper room of his house, the one with the windows that opened toward Jerusalem, and he prayed three times a day, as he always did. He simply thanked God for all the good things God had done for him. He knew that they would arrange to find him there in prayer one day, and they did. The witnesses went straight to the king and asked:

"Didn't you sign a decree that anyone who prayed to any god or man except you for thirty days would be thrown into the lions' den?"

"I certainly did, and the matter is sealed by the law of the Medes and Persians. It can't be revoked."

"Then what about your man, Daniel?" they asked him.

"What about Daniel?"

"Every day, three times a day, he ignores your decree and makes his prayers to his God."

The king was caught completely off guard. He had forgotten about Daniel! All the rest of the day he had his lawyers search for a loophole in the scheme. But he found none, and he had to admit that evening to the same delegation that there was no way to revoke an ordinance made by the king under the "Mede and Persian" clause. So he ordered Daniel to be taken to the royal lions' den.

"I pray that your God, Whom you serve so faithfully, can deliver you," Darius told Daniel as the guards pushed him into the den. Then a big stone was rolled over the entrance at the top, and the king set his seal on it in order that no one could open that den. So great was the king's concern for Daniel that he went back to the palace and spent the whole night fasting and praying in his fashion that no harm would come to Daniel.

As soon as day broke, the sleepless king went back to the lions' den. Even before he got to the den he called out, "Daniel, are you all right? Has your God Whom you serve been able to save you?" He could hardly believe his ears when he heard Daniel's voice:

"Don't worry, your majesty. My God sent an angel who shut the lions' mouths. God knows that I have done nothing wrong, and so do you."

"Get him out of there," the king commanded the guards. "I have another plan for feeding these lions. Bring the men who accused Daniel. Bring their families too. We'll throw the whole lot into the den to see how they make out."

They didn't do so well. Before they got to the bottom of the pit in the den they were torn apart by the hungry beasts.

Now Darius knew what Nebuchadrezzar and Belshazzar learned: that Daniel's God was the Lord to worship. So he put it into a decree that everybody should worship this God. Unfortunately, or fortunately, true worship can't be commanded by Law. People like Daniel continued their faithfulness through the reigns of both Darius and Cyrus who followed him.

Big Horns and
A Little One

Now Daniel is the one having the dreams.

After the stories in the first six chapters where Daniel was interpreting dreams for kings, the last six chapters replay some dreams and visions Daniel had of the future.

Maybe he was still thinking of his own interpretation of Nebuchadrezzar's dream about the image made of four kinds of metal, because his first dream in chapter 7 deals with the same four kingdoms. Belshazzer was still king of Babylon when Daniel got out of bed one night to write down the dream he had just witnessed in his sleep.

"I saw the ocean, with winds stirring it up, and four large beasts came up out of the sea. Each one was different from the other. The first one was like a lion, but it had wings of an eagle. But as I looked the wings were plucked off somehow, and the lion was lifted up and made to stand upright on two legs, like a human being. It started to think with the mind of a person.

"Then there was a second one, like a bear. Between its teeth there were three ribs, and a voice was saying to it 'Get up and eat a lot of meat.'

"A third one rose up, a leopard with four wings on its back. Also the animal had four heads. This one was ruler over everything it saw.

"And then the fourth. It was terrible and stronger than

any other beast. It had great iron teeth. Anything it wanted, it devoured, or stamped what was left into the ground with its feet. It had ten horns, and as I looked another one, a little one, grew up among them. To make room for it, three of the ten horns were pulled out by the roots. In this little horn were eyes, like the eyes of a person, and a mouth that was speaking.

"Suddenly, the scene changed. I saw thrones, as in a judgment hall. A Person who was as old as time, with pure white hair and dressed in pure white clothes, sat on a throne of flames. It had wheels of burning fire, and a stream of fire came out of the front of the throne. All the people who ever lived or will live stood before the throne, and the judgment books were opened. The little horn was still talking, and the whole beast was struck down. Its body was burned. But the other three, whose power was taken away, were still allowed to live on for a time.

"Now another figure appeared. Coming on clouds was a Person like a Human Being. He stood before the Ancient One, and to him was given all power and dominion over all nations and people. His kingdom would never pass away.

"I couldn't stand it. I approached one of the people standing there in the scene and asked: 'What does all this mean?' And this is what he said:

" 'The four beasts are four kings that will arise, but the saints of God will receive the kingdom that will finally last forever.' " (Jewish scholars identified the lion as Nebuchadrezzar and the Babylonian Empire, the bear as Media which tore the empire away from Babylon, the leopard as Persia, with four kings, and the terrible beast was the Seleucid Empire which controlled Palestine as well as the remnants of the other three empires. The little horn was Antiochus Epiphanes, who wrested the crown away from father and two brothers—the three uprooted horns. Alexander the Great, plus six successors before the father of Antiochus Epiphanes, may be the ten horns of the beast.)

The idea that a real Person would someday rule instead of beasts is a great insight for Daniel or anybody else. Creation was never intended to be governed by brute force, but by Human Beings made in the image of the Creator God. That, the *Genesis* story says, is why H.B. was put here.

"No sooner had my informant told me that 'the saints of God will receive the kingdom that will finally last forever,' than the Little Horn began to make war on the saints. He beat them, too, and ruled over them until God stepped in to return the kingdom to the People of God."

The dream description turns to poetry in verse 23, to repeat the information about the horns of the fourth beast. Some additional insights are given:

"The saints will be given into his hand (the little horn, Antiochus Epiphanes) for a time, two times, and half a time." Count a "time" as a year, and it turns out that the three and a half years mark the exact period between the erecting of the hated altar of Zeus and the restoration of the temple altar by the Maccabees.

"I looked in the mirror after writing down the dream, and I was still pale. It was a frightening dream," Daniel concluded. But the fright did not keep Daniel from dreaming. Chapter 8 recalls another one in which he dreamed he was in Susa, a large palace area on one side of Babylon, standing near the canal bank and looking at a ram which was also standing on the bank of the canal.

The ram had two large horns, but one was taller than

the other, though the longer one grew last. While he watched, the ram put on quite a show for Daniel. He charged to the west, then to the south and then to the north. (Perhaps if Daniel had realized that the ram, the Persian Empire with two divisions at first, Media and Persia, with Persia coming along to be the dominant of the two, also had moved in conquest all the way to central India, he would have had the ram take a charge toward the east as well.) Anyway, he was the he-ram that ruled to the four corners of their world.

Now a he-goat enters. He comes sailing in from the west, going so fast that his feet don't even touch the ground. He has one great horn between his eyes (horns, by the way, always denote power). Before the ram knew what was happening, the he-goat banged into him and shattered both the ram's horns. Under the goat's charge, the ram went down, and the goat stamped him into the ground. So the he-goat was king of the hill for a while. The Empire of Alexander expanded even more, until one day the big horn broke. And in place of the big horn, Alexander the Great, four smaller horns grew.

One of the four divisions of Alexander's world empire now produced a smaller horn which extended toward the south and east, and finally covered the Promised Land. The little horn magnified himself, even to the point of throwing down the altar of the Lord. He took over the sanctuary reserved for God alone, and stopped the burnt offerings from being offered to the Lord. Instead he ordered that they be made to his god, Zeus. He trampled on everything that was holy and right.

"How long can this go on?" Daniel heard a holy Being ask another. "How long is this 'abomination of desolation' going to be allowed in the temple?"

The other Being answered, "For two thousand and

three hundred evenings and mornings. Then the sanctuary will be restored to its rightful use." "In other words," Daniel said to himself, "there is a morning and evening in every day, so the time will be one thousand, a hundred and fifty days, which is a little over three years and two months."

"The rest of it," Daniel thought in his dream, "I need help on."

"Gabriel," a voice called from heaven to a man-like Being who now stood before Daniel, "see that this man understands this vision he is having."

When he heard that, Daniel prostrated himself on the ground before the one called Gabriel. And he heard him saying, "You have to understand that this vision refers to the end of time. So get up and listen." And here, chapter 8:20-26, the explanation comes that we wove into the story of the dream.

The first dream turned him pale with fright. This second one laid Daniel up sick in bed for several days. When he got up and went back to his business, he still felt appalled by the whole idea.

A prayer for his people was in order. His dreams had centered on the future of Israel, but what about their situation at the present time? Reading through old accounts of Jeremiah's speeches and writing, Daniel came across his prediction that the Babylonian captivity would last about seventy years. This was now the first year of Darius, the king of the Medes and Persians who had conquered Babylon (chapter 9). And Daniel felt the need for a prayer of confession on behalf of his people.

"O Lord, You keep the covenant of steadfast love with those who keep Your commandments, yet we have sinned and turned aside from Your commandments. We didn't listen to the prophets who spoke Your word to our rulers and to all the people, and now we are scattered among the nations and confused. The curse written out by Moses has been poured out upon us because of our sin. And yet we have not yet asked Your favor by turning from our iniquities and paying attention to Your truth. Now we admit it, and we throw ourselves again on Your mercy. You brought Your people out of Egypt; now do it again. Let Your anger turn away from Jerusalem, and look again with favor on the holy hill and Your sanctuary. We don't ask this because of our own righteousness, but because of Your great mercy. Help us for the sake of Your own name, because we are the people who are called by Your name. Amen.

"Well, before I was through praying one evening," Daniel said, "Gabriel showed up again."

"Daniel, you had no sooner started praying than I was dispatched to come here. You are a good man, and we are going to let you in on this mystery. Take the seventy years of Jeremiah and multiply it by seven. That's how long it will take to bring atonement for all the sins, and to set up the holy place. After the first seven of those 'weeks of years' (49 years) a prince shall come who will give the word to rebuild Jerusalem. Then for 434 more years of much trouble, Jerusalem and the temple will be rebuilt. That's sixty-nine weeks of years. Then comes the terrible seventieth. Once again a harsh conqueror will rule, culminating in the desolation of the altar of God by an abomination. For half a week (three and a half years) it will be there. Then God will put an end to it."

(The author's arithmetic was faulty when he calculated the 434-year period between Daniel's time and his own, but the message is clear. Long ago in another time of slavery in ancient Babylon and Persia, the vision had come that the end of the present seven years of horror would soon come to an end. So keep the faith, the faith of Daniel!)

Forget the chapter divisions from the beginning of chapter 10 to the end of the book. It is all one story, beginning in the third year of the reign of Cyrus. Daniel was mourning, fasting, and letting his whiskers grow for three weeks. Then another vision came. This time he was standing on the banks of the Tigris River where he saw a man clothed in linen, wearing a fine gold loin cloth imported from Ophir. His body was almost transparent, like beryl, with arms and legs like bronze, and a brilliant face with eyes like fire. When he spoke it was like thunder.

"There were other people with me in the vision," Daniel recalls, "and though they didn't see what I saw, they started to tremble and then they ran away. I didn't have any strength left in me to run. Instead, when he began to speak, I fell on my face in a deep sleep. A hand touched me, and I got to my hands and knees. It was the voice again that got me up on my feet.

" 'Stand upright, and don't be afraid. From the first day you set your mind to understand and obey God, you have been heard everytime you pray. That's why I have been sent to you. The guardian angel of Persia kept me away from you for twenty-one days, but Michael (guardian angel for the nation of Israel) came to help me, so I was able to come to tell you what is going to happen to your people in the days yet to come.'

"Again I bowed my head, and could not speak a word until another Human-like Being touched my lips. Then I said, 'I'm sorry, but this vision has sapped all the strength from me. I don't have breath enough to speak.' So he touched me again, and told me not to be afraid. I thanked him and told him I was ready to listen to anything he had to say.

" 'I have to return to fight against the prince of Persia,' he told me, 'and when I am through with him, the prince of Greece will come. See, we have the same troubles in heaven that you have here. All God's created Beings are not on the same side. The only one I have to fight with me against the angels of Persia and Greece is Michael, your prince or guardian angel. I helped Darius the Mede in his first year of overthrowing the Babylonian government, and now I can tell you truthfully that there will be three more kings in Persia. The last one of the three will be stronger and richer than the others. He will stir up a war against Greece, but that will be a mistake. The Great King (Alexander) will defeat him and rule all the earth. Then his kingdom will be divided into four. Ptolemy will be strong in his southern part of the empire, centering in Egypt, but one of his generals will take over the northern part, centering in Syria, and be even stronger. Some years later an alliance based on the marriage of the Seleucid king, Antiochus II of the north, to Berenice, a daughter of Ptolemy II, will fail to work. In fact, the woman, Laodice, whom Antiochus will divorce in order to marry Berenice, will have them assassinated, along with the son born to them. Her son, Seleucus II, will become king of the north, and Berenice's brother, Ptolemy III will come from the south to make war on Syria. Ptolemy III will capture the fortress at Antioch and take away a lot of booty to Egypt. For a while there will be no more attacks, until the king of the north makes one march on Egypt and then returns.' "

In verse 10 the review of history from Babylon to the time of the writer continues. The messenger from heaven is still telling Daniel the truth about "what is to come."

"The two sons who succeed Seleucus II, first Seleucus III and then Antiochus III, will keep up a running war with Egypt until (in 217 B.C.) Ptolemy IV inflicts a major defeat on the forces of the north. But, after some years, Antiochus will come back against the Egyptians to defeat them. At that time, some of your own people of Israel will try to hasten the coming of their freedom by rebelling against the king of the south. Antiochus will capture the well-fortified city of Sidon, and by 198 B.C. he will take all of Palestine away from the Ptolemy-part of Alexander's empire and make it all a part of the Seleucid portion. A peace treaty will involve Antiochus' daughter, Cleopatra, being married to Ptolemy V of Egypt.

"But disaster will come to Antiochus. Flush with victory over Egypt, he will turn west to attack the coastlands of Greece and Asia Minor, but a Roman commander (Scipio) will crush his troops in 190 B.C., take away all his westward conquests and send him home humiliated. Back home he will lose his life trying to loot the temple and fortress of Elam.

"Seleucus IV will follow his father. He will send an 'exactor of tribute through the glory of the kingdom' (that's Jerusalem and the temple), and he will take all the funds from the temple treasury. Then the 'exactor' will go home to conspire against Seleucus IV and have him killed. Now will come the most contemptible person of all, Antiochus IV Epiphanes, to take over the throne in Syria. Not only with armies, but with all kinds of underhanded schemes and bribery, he will try to win the favor of the people. He will even have a 'prince of the covenant' killed (high priest Onias), and will pay bribes like you have never seen to induce Jews to join his program of making everything Greek in their culture. In Egypt he will help one son of his sister, Cleopatra, in his fight against another son. Unable to force a decision there, he will return with a lot of booty. On his way home he will stop off in Jerusalem to put down a revolt and to steal more valuables from the temple itself.

"Later he will start an expedition to Egypt again, but on the way a fleet from Kittim (here meaning Rome probably) will intercept him and tell him to back off. Enraged, he will turn back to Judah. There he will end the sacrifices made in the temple, and set up in their place the statue of Zeus to whom all worship must be directed, the 'abomination of desolation.' Some people will go along with the new worship because of his bribes and his flattery, but many will remain true to the Lord God. They will withstand torture and death, and all kinds of persecution, and there won't be much help for them (not even from the rebel forces with the Maccabees). They will just have to suffer until the time comes for the end.

"Meanwhile, this vain little usurper will go around acting like he is God. Not only will he put down the worship of the true God, he will try to do away with the gods his own people have worshipped. He won't have any better sense than to try to get rid of the favorite gods of the women. And all this to establish in his region the worship of a god entirely foreign to the people— the Greek god, Zeus.

"Just before his end, the king of Egypt will attack, but Antiochus Epiphanes will meet him with great force, forces which will overrun all Palestine, except Edom and Moab and part of Ammon. He will continue on to conquer Egypt and all of north Africa, but a report of danger to his homeland from the east will draw him back to the coast of Palestine just west of Jerusalem. And there he will meet his end." (Here the author has left past history and is predicting what will happen in the months just ahead. The Jewish revolt against Antiochus Epiphanes was successful, but Antiochus never invaded

Egypt or north Africa. Apparently the writer didn't know that the Romans had drawn the line and warned Antiochus against any military venture to the south or west. The vision ends with the messenger saying:

"It will be Michael, Israel's guardian angel, who will do it. Your people will go through a traumatic experience, but they will be delivered. All those whose names are written in the book of life will be O.K. The people who stood firm and were wise enough not to desert God's side, and those who helped other people be righteous will come out shining like stars. Even many people who have died before that day will be resurrected. Some of them will be honored with more life; others will be facing shame and contempt.

"Now, Daniel, close this scroll and seal it until the right time to open it."

Apparently, the days of horror during the reign of Antiochus Epiphanes was the time to open it. That's how the writer got hold of it to pass it on for encouragement of the Jews of his day. But before he sealed it, Daniel had one more quick vision to record.

"I saw two men now, one on one bank of the river and the other on the opposite bank. I asked the man clothed in linen 'How long is it going to be before the wonderful end comes?' He raised his hands toward heaven and swore:

" 'By God, it will be a time, two times and half a time.' "

Daniel had received that same answer in the chapter 7 vision of the four beasts, so he tried again:

"But what is going to happen then?"

"You will just have to wait and see," the answer came. "At the end of time, the good people will understand, but the wicked people never will. Just rest patiently in your grave; you will be assured of a place in God's new kingdom at the end of the age."

In the Hebrew *Bible*, and in Protestant Bibles, the book of *Daniel* ends here. Roman Catholic versions, following the Greek Old Testaments, add as chapters 13 and 14 the two books, *Susanna* and *Bel and the Dragon*, which are found only in the *Apocrypha* for Protestants.

In *Susanna*, a lovely woman by that name is cleared of a false charge of adultery by a very brave and clever young man named Daniel. The story says that this "case" started his great reputation.

In the first part of *Bel and the Dragon*, Daniel exposes the tricks played on the people who think that their Babylonian God, Bel, actually eats the food they set before him as offering. In the second part, Daniel refuses to worship a great dragon, and actually kills it with a mixture of fat, hair and pitch. The people are so angry about their god's death that they demand that Daniel be thrown in the lion's den where he stays, unharmed, for six days. Finally, the king pulls Daniel out and throws his enemies in.

As we might expect, religious thought had changed in some respects over the four centuries that passed between the writing of the old prophets and this writing of the Daniel stories. For one thing, angels have names now. Nowhere else in the Old Testament (only in the *Apocrypha*) is an angel named, but here we met Gabriel and Michael. Of course, it may be a good thing if a person can get to know some angels by name. They seem to be of considerable help.

Another development lies in the faith concerning life after death. Up to now, the Old Testament idea of Sheol as a vague place for spirit bodies to go after death was all anyone dared hope for. Now the fact of a resurrection, with new life beyond this physical phase of life, is announced with certainty. It's too bad that we don't know who first accepted that idea, but it just reminds us that we have only a few books, and know only of a few persons among the many H.B.s who helped to develop the religious ideas we take for granted today. So, for all those other Daniels and Susannas we never heard about, we give thanks.

HOSEA

The One-Sided Love Affair

If *Daniel* were written today, Hosea would have been writing about 1385 A.D. That's how far the reader jumps back in time when he/she turns the page from *Daniel* to *Hosea* in the *Bible*. However, spiritually and ethically, there is no regression. Hosea's concerns and insights were every bit as modern as the writers six centuries later.

Jeroboam II, the son of Joash, was king of the northern kingdom of Israel when his 41-year term of prosperity and loose living was challenged by Amos, the first of the great ethical prophets. Before the end of his reign, he had another prophet of the same persuasion begin his preaching career. Hosea, or Hoshea, short for Jehoshua which is translated Joshua in English (and 'Jesus' in the New Testament) was his name. Hosea kept on preaching in the days of turmoil which followed Jeroboam II as the kings of Judah invited great Assyria to get Syria and Israel off their backs, an invitation that was to bring a terrible end to Israel forever.

The first words the Lord ever spoke to Hosea, according to Hosea himself, were quite unexpected:

"Go find a prostitute and marry her, and have children by her."

"Lord," Hosea said, "what would be the point of doing that?"

"This whole nation is committing adultery every day with foreign gods, so I want to give them an illustration they cannot ignore. The preacher marrying the prostitute will get their attention."

The woman's name was Gomer, and their first child's name was Jezreel. The Lord suggested that name because Hosea was to announce that the house of Jehu, current rulers of Israel, would be punished for the slaughter at Jezreel when Jehu overthrew Israel's ruling family and started his own dynasty. Also, the Lord had in mind that Israel's final defeat would come in the valley of Jezreel.

Child number 2 was a daughter, to be called "Not Pitied", because God would no more have pity on Israel. Judah, yes, but Israel? No. A third child's name carried a similar message: "Not My People." The covenant ties are not going to bind God to Israel any longer.

"Now, there will come a time in the future when Israel will be multiplied again, and instead of 'You Are NOT My People,' their name will be 'People of The Living God.' Israel and Judah will be reunited in one kingdom with one head, and the day of Jezreel will be one of victory, not defeat. So the son's name will be 'My People,' and the daughter's name will be 'She Has Obtained Pity.'

"But," the Lord continued, "for now your message must be that I am no longer husband to Israel, unless she puts away her adultery. If she does not, I will leave her stripped and without any provisions in the wilderness. The children of Israel will have no pity shown them because the nation has said, 'I will go after other lovers who will support me.' The only thing left for Me to do is to let her find out how little help they will be to her. Then, maybe, she will decide it is better to trust Me, her first husband. Perhaps then she will realize that it is I Who give the grain and the goods which the people have attributed to Baal.

"Meanwhile, I will just have to withhold the food and clothes, and her other lover-nations can see just how poor and naked she is. Since she thinks that her orchards and vineyards are gifts of other gods whom she has served as cult-priestess, I will make them overrun with weeds and growth so dense that animals will take them over. When she sees that the other gods are not able to take care of her, I will meet her in the wilderness and we will start our relationship all over again. Once again, I will build up her vineyards. The valley of Achor (trouble and despair before) will be a door of hope. We will be as we were when she came with Me out of the land of Egypt.

"Once again, you (because when I said 'she' I was talking to you, Israel) will call Me your husband. You won't even use the word 'Baal' anymore. I will make a new covenant with you, and seal it with perfect order in nature and in all human relationships. This time the proofs of our covenant will be seen in your righteousness and justice, steadfast love and mercy. For this is true faith. And you will know that the fertility of the earth comes only from Me, in rain from the sky, and earth that responds with crops of grain, wine and oil. I will plant 'Jezreel' in this land, have pity on 'Not Pitied,' and say to 'Not My People', you are My people. And they will all reply to Me, 'You are our God.' "

Nice thought, but chapter 3 takes us back to face the fact that right now Israel is playing the harlot, going after other gods as a wanton woman goes after other lovers even though she is married. And it will take a while for that kind of behavior to be changed. It is hard to tell whether the Lord is talking to Hosea about his wife,

Gomer, who has left him for others, or about taking a new wife who currently is either an adulteress or a cult-priestess, part of whose duties were to be a temple prostitute. At any rate, he has to pay the price of a slave (half in silver and half in barley) to take the woman home as his own wife.

"I will be faithful to you," Hosea told her, "and you will have to live here with me alone until you learn to love me truly."

"Just as it takes a while to reeducate her away from practicing a fertility-cult religion that uses pillars of stone, and ephods and household gods, so it will take a while for Israel to be stripped of leadership, exiled in other lands, until they return to seek Me alone," the Lord reminded Hosea.

If you want a "bill of particulars," these are the things God has against the people of Israel:

"No faithfulness or kindness;
no knowledge of God;
swearing, lying, killing, stealing, committing
adultery.

"That's why the drought comes to dry up the land and streams. It's not really the fault of the people; it is the fault of the leaders. Priests who should have been teaching the Law have not done it. They have greedily profiteered from the system of offering sacrifices on behalf of the people. They will have to pay for their deeds.

"The whole business of Baal worship is not only worthless; it is crazy. The acts of harlotry, the sexual fertility acts carried on at the shrines, don't produce any crops or animals, or any more babies. The spirits they drink don't bring the Spirit with any new understanding. In fact, the drink takes away understanding. They set up idols of wood and then ask them for help. They set up 'secret' and magical rites of worship in the woods and on the hilltops, but they find no meaning at all in any of it. Fathers let their daughters work as cult prostitutes in the name of Baal worship; husbands give their wives for it. I am not going to hold the women guilty. It is the men who set up this business and use them, and they will be punished. (At least, God tells Hosea that a double standard of morality is not going to allow men to get away with sexual looseness while women are supposed to be chaste.)

"At least try to keep Judah from being as false in its religion as Israel is," the Lord told Hosea. "Stay away from the mock religion of Gilgal and Bethaven. (Let's not call it 'Bethel—house of God.' Call it what it is: 'Bethaven—house of evil.') Israel is like a stubborn heifer, so I can't treat her as if she were a gentle lamb in a pasture. Ephraim (Hosea's way of referring to Israel) is too far gone to merit your attention. A bunch of drunks who prefer shame to glory, they will know what shame is when My wind of destruction sweeps away their altars."

In chapter 5, the prophet again hits the priests, the leaders of government, and the ruling house of Israel for leading the people astray in promoting false worship at the cult centers like Mizpah, Tabor and Shittim. Now the people of Israel are doing things that keep them from returning to God. Even if they come with their animals to sacrifice, the Lord will not be there to receive them. In their cult sexual practices they have given birth to children who have no knowledge of the true God. Their new moon holidays will turn to times of disaster.

"Sound the alarm in the border town of Israel; Judah is moving north past her border markers (answering the pressure from Syria and Israel combined), but God will punish Judah as well as Israel. Sending to Assyria to ask aid of the great king, Tiglath-Pileser III, is not going to be any cure for Judah's sickness. In fact, the cure will be worse than the problem for both little nations. And when Assyria comes like a lion to tear apart and carry away captives, it really will be the work of the Lord of Israel Who now is going to do nothing at all to help."

But Hosea follows that pronouncement of doom with what may be read as an act of repentance. Actually, we catch the sarcasm of his repeating what the people say, "Come, let us return to the Lord so we can be healed. God has punished us, now God will bind us up. We can count on being revived after a short time. Like the Baal god who dies and then comes back to us in the spring showers every year, the Lord will refresh us again."

The Lord sees through all that feigned repentance, however.

"What shall I do with you, Ephriam and Judah?" God asks wistfully. "Your love is like morning fog or dew that soon disappears. I hammer you with the words of My prophets; My judgments are as clear as light. How can you not know that all I want is your love, not your sacrifices? Knowing Me personally is better than making burnt offerings.

"Unfortunately," God continues, "ever since the people of Israel under Joshua crossed the Jordan at Adam (check *Joshua* 3) they have been breaking our covenant. Gilead is a city filled with evil doers. Even the priests are not above murder; the nation practices harlotry everywhere."

"When the Lord tries to heal Israel and restore her fortunes," Hosea continues (chapter 7), "all the wicked deeds are revealed and God can't ignore them. The king's own household takes the lead in debauchery. There is no peace or rest from the constant turmoil that greed and passion bring. Like a baker's fire in the oven that is only banked at night, to be stirred to blaze again in the morning, constant intrigue goes on. New rulers come and soon fall to the drunken conspirators who plot to put a new king on the hill. And through it all, none of them calls on the Lord God.

"As bad as domestic affairs are, Israel's foreign policy is even more half-baked. Aliens are eating Israel up. But false pride keeps Israel from admitting its need to return to God. No, Israel is like a silly dove that flits between Egypt and Assyria. Some day the Lord will snare this bird in the net. The Lord would redeem Israel, but they have no truth in them. Instead of crying out from the heart to the true God, they wail in the religious rites over the dying god, even gashing themselves as they beg for the return of spring vegetation. It was the Lord God who trained and strengthened the warriors of Israel, but they turned to worship Baal. Now they will fall by the sword, and return once more to captivity they had in Egypt."

The prophet sees in chapter 8 the vulture wheeling around Israel's house. The circling buzzard was Assyria, which would soon descend because the divine death sentence has been passed on the nation. Two reasons are given for the sentence: kings have been selected without God's approval, and idols have been set up for worship. Ever since Jeroboam set up those golden bulls to keep the people of Israel from going down to Jerusalem's temple to worship, the Lord has been extremely displeased. That golden calf is going to be smashed to pieces.

" 'They sow the wind, and they shall reap the whirlwind,' as the old proverb says," Hosea continued. "Sowing nothing, Israel will reap nothing, and even that nothing is going to be swallowed up by aliens. Already Israel ranks as nothing among the nations because it has gone to Assyria for its gods, not trusting its own God. The word Ephriam is awful close to the word for 'wild ass,' and that's what Ephraim is. God will soon erase Israel from the list of nations, and they won't have to keep anointing one new king after another.

"The more altars they build, the more they sin. They love sacrifices but the teaching of God they don't even recognize. They love to sacrifice animals (and eat the meat too, of course); but the Lord doesn't care one bit for any of that stuff. What God does see is their sin and wrongdoing, and for that they will be punished. Their trust in their material possessions and military power is a poor substitute for trust in their Creator God. So back to bondage they will go."

The last six chapters are a collection of more comments and parts of sermons that Hosea preached during the years before Assyria wiped out Israel, deporting the people to other parts of their empire. The "ten lost tribes of Israel" would never return because they never answered the appeal of Amos and Hosea to change their idolatrous ways. Over and over he hits the theme: "Israel has played the harlot. Forsaking God, the men of Israel have given themselves to the fertility rites where they engage in sexual acts with cult prostitutes in order to appeal to the Baal who were supposed to control the renewal of crops each spring. By now you should know that such foolishness will not produce any grain or wine," Hosea says. "It only degrades the character of our nation and makes it impossible for the Lord to help us." That's point number 1.

Point number 2 is also made again and again:

"Sacrifices of animals and grain and wine do not

please the Lord. Tainted by their worship of foreign gods, the food they offer is all unclean anyway. Getting rid of all the idols and religious trappings that indicate their love for other gods, and creating relationships based on justice and righteousness, is the only way to please the Lord God of Israel.

"For not listening to point 2, the nation is going to be driven into slavery once again." That's point 3. "It may be Egypt again; it may be Assyria this time, but the Lord cannot allow this conduct to continue. Instead of the prosperity Israel has enjoyed, at least the rich people have, there will be briar patches instead of great estates. And those days are coming soon."

What reward does the prophet of God get for all his efforts? He is called a fool; they say that he is crazy; they express their hatred toward him, even in the house of God, because their own sin is so great. They are always trying to nail him for breaking some law. But the prophet is a voice of conscience in Israel, a reminder of their God, so he cannot back off. Hosea will have to keep telling the truth: that punishment is coming from God because the people have corrupted themselves (9:7-17). They are as bad now as the men of Gibeah whose lust left the Levite's concubine dead in the *Judges* story.

Even with a covenant with God, the people of Israel still turned to worship of Baal because their greatest attention was given to their own crops and material prosperity. In name they stayed the People of God. In fact they became the people of Baal. It is a process that continues in all of H.B.'s history, including the future, no doubt. H.B. becomes like that to which she/he pays most attention. Whatever is first place in our thought and desire is really our god. So God welcomed our ancestors as eagerly as a traveler in the desert welcomes an oasis with fresh fruit, but Israel's side of the covenant was never kept.

"Now Ephraim will see that the Baal cannot produce. It is God Who has been blessing Israel all along, and now God's care is finally going to be removed. There will be no more fertility, and children that do come along will be taken away or killed until none are left. Ever since they crossed into the Promised Land with Joshua at Gilgal they began to try the Lord's patience. Now they have become so wicked that God will drive them out to be outcasts among other nations.

Prosperity did not turn My people in thanksgiving to Me," the Lord had Hosea say. "The richer they became, the more they built their own altars and the more they felt independent of Me." (How "modern" do we want these old prophets to be?) "Now I will have to break down their altars and show them how mistaken they are."

"So," Hosea preached, "judgment springs up like poisonous weeds in a plowed field. It's bound to come, and when it does the priests will wail and the people will tremble as the awful calf of Bethel is carried away to Assyria as part of the loot taken by the great Assyrian king. Then Israel will be ashamed of its idol. The little pipsqueak king of Israel will have about as much influence on events as a wood chip on the surface of the ocean. The 'high places' where Israel has practiced its idolatrous worship will be destroyed; briars and thistles will grow in place of their altars. And people will be praying for the mountains to fall on them before something worse happens to them. After all, they have piled up a mountain of iniquity across the centuries.

"Instead of the easier life of treading out grain, eating what it wanted, Israel will now be a heifer yoked to the hard work of plowing and harrowing the fields. If only the nation would sow righteousness, it would reap the fruit of God's love! If only the people would seek the Lord instead of Baal, the saving rain would come from God! But no, you planted sin and you reaped injustice, and now you will eat the fruit of your lies. You trusted in your military might, and now your land will be destroyed by greater military might. What happened to Beth-arbel when it was crushed, with mothers and children slaughtered, will happen to the house of Israel, and the king of Israel will be cut off."

Chapter 11 opens with a passage *Matthew* later applied to the baby Jesus. He was using "proof texts" the way some preachers still use them today. Hosea is referring to God's calling Israel out of Egypt in the exodus, and then having to see Israel turn away to worship Baals and idols. So blind and dumb were the people of Israel that they couldn't see that it was God Who took care of them, teaching them, healing them, leading them with love and kindness. Now they must go back to slavery, this time in Assyria. War will ravage their country because they will not return to the Lord.

It isn't an easy thing for God to do. Hosea pictures God as grieving over the loss of Israel.

"How can I give you up, Ephraim! How can I hand you over, O Israel! How can I destroy you! My heart recoils from the very thought. Never again will I destroy the nation, because I simply cannot operate with complete vengeance as human beings sometimes do. I am not here to destroy completely. After a time, the scattered people of Israel will return like homing pigeons from Egypt and Assyria, and I will bring them back to their homes. Even now some in Judah are remaining loyal to Me, but Israel is like a rich trader who swindles people to gain his wealth. His riches can never pay for the guilt he amassed while getting the riches. So he must actually live in tents, instead of just having the week-long "feast of booths" where families set up a tent in the back yard to remind themselves of the exodus time in the desert.

"You know, there really is no excuse for Israel's lostness. I gave them a prophet to lead them out of Egypt, and prophets to preserve their religion in this land. Still, Israel has constantly provoked My anger."

"It's too bad," Hosea adds (chapter 13). "Ephraim, son of Joseph, was the main man in the ten tribes of Israel. But his going after Baal killed him spiritually. Now his people sin more and more, making molten images and idols. . .even kissing golden calves. Go out and watch the morning mist leave the valley, or see the winds blow chaff away from the grain which is being threshed, or blow smoke out of a window, and you will know what happens to H.B. when he/she forsakes the Lord."

"When they were hungry they needed Me," the Lord told Hosea. "But when they got their bellies full, they forgot Me. Now instead of taking care of them, I will be like a lion or leopard ready to ambush them along the trail. A she-bear robbed of her cubs would be no greater threat to tear them apart than I. And who will be there to save them? They said they wanted kings and princes, not trusting Me any more to lead them. I gave them their kings, and now I am taking them away. I offer them the chance to be reborn, but they refuse.

"So the east wind is rising in the wilderness, and Assyria comes to dry up the proud plant that is Israel. Everything in the land will be stripped clean, and all the riches of the treasury will be taken away. Because of their rebellion against God, the people will be cut down by the sword of the conqueror, even little children and pregnant women."

But the last chapter represents one last appeal for repentance. It seems that this is always the final word of the true prophet because even God's punishment is aimed at rehabilitation, not retribution.

"If you seek Me with all your heart, you shall surely find Me," Jeremiah later echoed Hosea who urged Israel to sincerely repent and return to the Lord. "Quit your wickedness, do what is right and good, and speak sincerely. Stop aping Assyria, put away your idol worship, and be merciful to orphaned children and those who are helpless. Then see how God's anger turns away from you. The loving divine Presence will be like dew to parched ground, and Israel will grow and bear fruit again. It will be an oasis of trees and fruit, all the fertility the Baal promised and couldn't deliver.

"Why can't you wise up and see this: the ways of the Lord are good. If we walk in them we will get results. If we try to go other ways, we will have to take the consequences. Take your choice."

JOEL

Valley of Decision

Was he one of the Joels mentioned elsewhere in the Old Testament? We don't know.

Did he live in or near Jerusalem? Probably.

Isn't it likely that he was writing sometime after the rebuilding of Jerusalem and the temple following the Babylonian exile? Yes. When we turned the page from *Daniel* to *Hosea*, we stepped back six hundred years. Now from *Hosea* to *Joel* we move forward about four centuries. So prepare to shift mental gears again.

What seemed to prompt the writing? A swarm of locusts and grasshoppers. A cloud of grasshoppers is even today apt to bring a good many remarks from a farmer. Maybe Joel had a garden that was eaten up by them. At any rate, he used the hopper invasion to warn his people that this may be only the prelude to that great Judgment Day of the Lord. So don't put off repentance and setting the house in order.

"Do you see what is happening here?" Joel asked the men and women around him. "Ask the oldest people if they have ever heard their ancestors mention such a thing. This is something we will tell our children about, and our children's great grandchildren will be telling their great grandchildren about it!

"You think this is just another dry season with the

locusts worse than usual? Think again. What the cutting locust left, the swarming locust ate. What the swarming locust left, the hopping locust devoured. And what the hopping locust missed, the destroying locust cleaned up. I'm telling you that the first people to complain will be the winos. The vines are all gone and there will be no grape juice this season. They will put up a wail about that.

"This is worse than an invasion of a human army. The soldiers in this invasion are countless; they eat their way through the land, stripping bare the vines and fig trees. Priests will join the wine drinkers in their lament, because there isn't enough produce to keep the sacrificial offerings going in the temple. The farmers can tell them that. Maybe the priests had better put on their sackcloth and call the people together for a day of fasting, because this may well be the beginning of the Day of the Lord. We know that destruction will come with God's Judgment, and how much more effectively could the Lord begin to deal it out? Right before our eyes, our entire food supply is being cut off! There is no grass, no grain, and soon there will be no animals. Pastures and fields are burning up because everything is so dry."

In chapter 2, Joel pictures God as sounding the alarm:

"Blow the trumpet on Mount Zion, so that everyone will tremble to know that the Day of the Lord is near; it is a day of judgment and gloom worse than anything seen by the old timers or by the generations to come. This Promised Land, your Garden of Eden, will be left a burned-over, desolate wilderness. Look at them, and you will see how these locusts are like war horses covering the mountains. Listen to them; they sound like the rumbling of chariots. When they eat their way through a field it sounds like the crackling of a flame as it burns the stubble. They swarm over a town like an army scaling the walls. They march straight ahead in columns like well-disciplined troops. No weapons can halt their attack. They climb over walls and houses, pouring through windows and doors as silently as thieves. The whole earth shakes before them; they darken the skies as they come over in clouds. They are My army, and they do My command.

"Yet even now," the Lord says, "you can return to Me with your whole heart. Change your hearts instead of tearing your clothes. Let Me see some real sorrow and repentance on your part."

"Don't you see how this locust infestation is God's call to us?" Joel tried to emphasize. "Come back to the Lord, your God; the Lord is gracious and merciful, slow to anger, and full of steadfast love. God doesn't want to hurt us. And if we will repent sincerely, this tragedy may come to an end and we can once again sacrifice our food offerings in the temple.

"We ought to call a national assembly right now. Everybody in the country—men, women and children, even bridal couples just married—must be there. The priests, who will be stationed as usual between the burnt-offering altar and the entrance, can pray for us. They can ask God to spare us so that other nations won't have the chance to ridicule the Lord by saying 'Where is their God? Can't their God take care of them?' "

Now draw a line after verse 17 of chapter 2. The last half of the little book assumes that the nation will repent. So from here on there are promises from the Lord for better days. And if they had happened like this, Joel's idea that nothing like it would ever be seen again would be wonderfully true.

"I'm calling off the locust army. They will die in the desert and there will be a stench from the Mediterranean to the Dead Sea. People and animals can relax. Pastures will be green again; fruit trees and vines will yield their fruit once more. The early rain (fall) and the latter rain (spring) will be abundant. You will have a great harvest of grain and fruit, and it will more than make up for all the damage done by the great army of locusts.

"You will have plenty to eat, so you will praise Me again. I won't ever put you to shame again, but you will know that I am the Lord, and there is no other God to whom you can turn."

Physical blessings will only mark the beginning of the new day. Now comes an even greater promise from the Lord (beginning with verse 28):

"I am going to pour out My Spirit on you. Both men and women will be prophets. Your old people will dream dreams; your young people will see visions. (There always seem to be a connection between the dreaming of dreams on the part of adults and the seeing of visions on the part of youth.) Servants will share this gift as well as their masters."

Peter was, four centuries later, to use this last section of Joel, chapter 2, to try to explain what was happening on the Day of Pentecost following the resurrection of Jesus. Perhaps the promise is for H.B. anytime and anywhere he/she is ready to open up to receive it.

The cosmic signs that had always been associated with the Day of the Lord are promised also: "fire and smoke, the sun darkened, the moon red as blood (with smoke so dense from the fires?). But everyone who serves the Lord will find sanctuary in Jerusalem. Those whom the Lord calls will be saved because they will know where to put their trust."

The promises continue:

"I will restore the fortunes of Jerusalem and Judah.

I will gather all the nations in the valley of Jehoshaphat (not necessarily a specific valley, but a place of God's judgment) and they will be judged according to how they treated the people of Israel during time of exile. Some of them sold the Jews as slaves as if they were pieces of property to be divided out by flipping a coin; they bought and sold boys and girls for a bottle of wine or a visit with a prostitute."

One illustration of that crime is given in 3:4-8, which may have been a later addition to the text. The forces of Tyre and Sidon, in league with the Philistines, looted Judah of its treasures and sold many of its people as slaves to the Greeks. But the Jews will get their turn to take their enemies as slaves and sell them to the Sabeans who will take them across the Arabian desert.

Back to the call to assemble the nations in the valley of judgment. Beginning in verse 9, we have a surprising switch to the beautiful prophecy of both *Isaiah* 2:4 and *Micah* 4:3. They saw this final judgment day of the nations as a day for "beating swords into plowshares, and spears into pruning hooks," with nations giving up warfare altogether. Joel says that they will "beat their plowshares into swords, and their pruning hooks into spears; let even the weak person say 'I am a warrior.' " Let the nations come as armies into the valley of decision, and there they will perish by the sword as they have taken the sword. Once and for all Judah is going to be delivered from her oppressors, free to live at Mt. Zion and worship the Lord, separate from aliens and holy before God.

"What a Utopia that will be! The hills will practically flow with wine and milk, and the stream that flows from the temple in Ezekiel's vision will water all the valley toward the Dead Sea. The traditional enemies of Israel,

Edom and Egypt, will be left desolate because of what they have done to Israel in the past. But Judah will be prosperous and peaceful forever."

It is a dream many Jews today would still like to see come true. It may be that they must join with all the rest of us H.B.s on the earth in understanding that until all Edoms and Egypts share the peace and prosperity promised to Judah, none of us will have it permanently. The question of plowshares or swords, bread or bullets, is still to be settled in the valley of decision to which God calls all nations.

AMOS

The Trailblazer

He was the first prophet to have his words written down and kept as a collection of his messages. And he was the first in the line of great prophets who came in the eighth century B.C. to raise to a new plateau the level of H.B.'s perception of what God wants. When we stand with Amos we stand at the threshold of a new era in our religious thought. We have once again moved backward in Old Testament history four hundred years from the book of *Joel*. And Joel probably knew how much he was influenced by Amos and the great ethical prophets who had plowed their insights deep into Jewish understanding.

Years later Zechariah 14:5 referred to the great earthquake that shook Israel during the reign of King Uzziah in Judah. In the days just preceding that event, a sheepman from Tekoa, ten miles south of Jerusalem, felt called by the Lord to speak out publicly against some of the religious and social life of Israel and Judah. The writer summarizes Amos' message in the second verse of chapter one:

"The Lord's word from Mt. Zion is clear as thunder. Prosperity is over; the day of death is coming."

For a look at how, and when and where he said that, we can imagine Amos standing in a prominent place in a city of Samaria holding the attention of a crowd of citizens of Israel as he speaks in tones that carry to the corners of the square.

"Thus says the Lord," he begins. And every ear gives attention because only a few of the prophets of the Lord God use that pattern of speech. "Thus says the Lord:

"You want to know what is going to happen to Damascus and the Syrians? For all of their transgressions against Me, I am going to let punishment come to them. You remember what they did to the prisoners in Gilead, just east of us? They rolled iron-toothed threshing sledges over them. So I am going to burn up the ruling house of Syria, tear down their defenses, kill the king, and send the people of Syria back into exile in Kir (like telling the Israelites they were going back to slavery in Egypt). That's what the Lord says."

"Right on!" somebody probably shouted from the crowd. "We've been waiting for years to hear that!"

"Thus says the Lord," (Amos was continuing his speech) "for all the wicked deeds of Gaza, and the other Philistine cities of Ashdod, Ashkelon, and Ekron, I will bring punishment. Because they sold many people for slaves to Arabian traders, they will be destroyed."

This time there is applause. The crowd is "with him." This is good preaching.

"Thus says the Lord, Tyre is going to catch the punishment too. They sold people into slavery; they broke treaties with their neighbors. So their walls will be broken down and the city burned."

Applause again.

Amos pauses for effect, then says again: "Thus says the Lord, for all the bad things Edom has done, I will punish them also. They have torn at Judah every chance they got, never showing pity. Now their strongholds will be torn down. Edom will be smashed!"

"Amen, preacher! Let's hear more."

"Thus says the Lord:

"The Ammonites are doomed as well. They came into Gilead and ripped up pregnant women. And you know of other crimes they have committed. Their capital city of Rabbah will look as if a tornado has destroyed it after conquerors are through with their attack. The king and leading people will be taken away as captives."

"And so will Moab," Amos hurried on. "Thus says the Lord: I will not keep Moab from punishment either, because of all the transgressions of that nation. Remember the terrible act of burning the revered bones of Edom's king in their national shrine? So their king will die, and all the leaders with him. The whole nation will die with no burial place."

All the buzz in the public square had ceased now. Every ear was tuned to this rough prophet who was predicting woe for their enemies. Again he spoke.

"Thus says the Lord. For the three transgressions of Judah, and for four, I will not turn back the punishment."

"Judah is going to be punished too?" they gasped.

"Yes. Judah has rejected the Law of the Lord; they have not kept God's commandments. Their false gods have led them astray. So Judah is on the hit list too. Jerusalem will be destroyed."

"That's a strong thing to say at the end of the sermon," some of them were thinking. But Amos wasn't through. Pausing only to let the effect of what he had just said about their brothers and sisters in Judah sink in, Amos spoke out even louder:

"Thus says the Lord: For all the sins of Israel the punishment will come! Because they exploit the poor and innocent people, selling poor people into slavery when they can't pay off the debt for a pair of shoes; because they trample the poor into the dust, and completely disregard the needs of helpless people; because both a father and his son commit the fertility cult sex act with the same girl, bringing shame to the name of God; because they commit these acts at pagan altars while lying on clothes the poor people had to pawn; and because they drink wine paid for by taxes laid on needy people, they are going to be destroyed."

The murmuring of the crowd only forced Amos to say more.

"God destroyed the Amorites who opposed Israel's coming into this land, and they were a strong nation. God brought Israel out of Egypt, led them for forty years in the wilderness, and brought them in to possess the country. God raised up some of Israel's sons and daughters to be prophets, and some of your young men to be Nazarites. Isn't that right? You know it is. But you made the Nazarites who were sworn to abstinence drink wine, and you refused to let the prophets be free to speak for God!

"No, you cannot escape the awful pressure of God's judgment. Even the swiftest cannot run fast enough, nor can the strongest save themselves. Not even a person on horseback can escape the terror that is coming to Israel!''

Perhaps the noise of the suddenly-angered crowd drowned out his sermon at this point, but, beginning with chapter 3, the shepherd-prophet found ways to say and write more details of his message from the Lord to the people of Israel.

"You know why God is going to be harder on you than on all the other nations who disregard God's ways? It's because you were the favored nation, and more was expected of you. How do I know this is true? Well, let me ask you:

"Do two people travel together unless they have agreed to do it?

"Does a lion roar in the forest when there is nothing to kill, or the lion's cub growl with pleasure when it is eating nothing?

"Does a bird get caught in a snare when no trap has been set?

"Does a trap spring shut when nothing has triggered it?

"Does a warning trumpet blow in a city without frightening the people?

"Does evil come to a place unless God has done it?

"So your sin and God's judgment go hand in hand. How can I say otherwise? I know what the lion's roar means, and I can't help telling you!

"Gather round all the traditional enemies of Israel; let them see the things that are going on in Samaria. They will see why the Lord says 'these people don't know what right is; they gain their wealth by violence and oppression.'

"Therefore, thus says the Lord: the army of the invader (Assyria was coming) is going to break down your strongholds and plunder this land. As a shepherd, I have rescued from a lion small bits of a sheep that was killed and eaten. That's about all that will be left of Israel. If a resident of Samaria gets away with the corner of a couch or part of a bed, he or she will be lucky.

"All the altars, even Bethel's, in which you put your trust will be torn down. There won't be any horns on the big altar for anyone to hold and beg for mercy. Your fine houses and your summer cottages in the country, with all their expensive furnishings will be destroyed.

The ivory of their inlaid paneling will be about as much value to you as it is to the elephants that were slaughtered to get it.

"And speaking of elephants, hear this word, you cows of Bashan—yes, I mean you, you 'ladies' of Samaria who are sleek and well fed like the fat cattle on your ranches—you join with your husbands in robbing the poor people, showing no mercy on the needy. The only thing you care about is the money coming in so you can continue to party. By all that is holy, the Lord is going to see that the days are coming when you will be dragged away from the city with hooks in your mouths as captives. They won't even have to take you through the gates; the walls will be so torn up that you can walk straight out of town in any direction. If you don't live through the ordeal, they will drag your carcasses to the dump."

It is a safe bet that Amos was not asked to return the next week to "lead the devotions" at the Ladies Tea and Bingo Circle. Nor was he a popular speaker to rally the churchgoers for more sacrificial giving, not after his two-verse sermon in chapter 4 (verses 4 and 5):

"Come on up to the shrine at Bethel, everybody. Come up and multiply your sins! Bring your animal and food sacrifices every morning, and don't forget your tithes. Oh, and make sure everybody knows how big your free-will offerings are. You people of Israel just love to make a show of your religion, don't you?"

When he settled down to good, straightforward warning, he set the tone for the remarks of all the great prophets who followed him as they analyzed the situation as the Lord saw it:

"I tried taking everything away from you, even to the point of starvation, but you still didn't come back to Me for help. I tried holding back the rain, or sometimes letting it rain in one area to point up how dry it was in another, but you still didn't get the point. I tried ruining your crops with blight, mildew and locusts, but that didn't work either. I even allowed your young men to be killed in war, with the stench of rotting bodies smelling up your country, but you still would not return to Me. Even the ones of you who were saved, like brands pulled out of a fire before they were burned up, when some of your cities have fallen like Sodom and Gomorrah, did not repent and acknowledge Me as Lord.

"Therefore, (watch out when a true prophet gets to the 'therefore,') "prepare to meet your God. This is no trivial judgment you face. God Who created all there is, including human beings, the Lord God Almighty is passing this sentence on Israel: 'You shall fall, never again to rise. You will be lucky to have a tenth of your people left after the coming battles.' "

Amos always added, "Of course, if you seek God sincerely you will live, but the kind of so-called worship you do at Bethel, Gilgal, or even down at Beer-sheba in Judah, will not get you one bit of help. Seek the Lord and live, or be ready for the fire that will burn up the house of Israel. It is surely coming to you who turn justice into a bitter experience, and tear down anything that is right or good!"

Amos couldn't understand how anyone could deliberately snub the Lord Who is the one Creator and Sustainer of all the cosmos. His line of reasoning and some of his beautiful language was used again and again by speakers and writers who came in the years following.

"God who made the Pleiades and Orion and the other starry constellations, Who turns darkness into morning and light into darkness, Who brings rain to the thirsty earth, also controls human destiny. No human being is strong enough to withstand divine judgment.

"That is why the people who exploit the poor, and who resent it when the truth is told about them in the city court at the gate, don't want to face the God of justice. They cheat and steal from the poor in order to build fine houses for themselves. But they won't have them very long to live in," Amos announced. "You planted vineyards too, but you won't be around to drink their wine, because the Lord knows how insensitive and wicked you are. Your only hope is to seek the Lord, change from loving evil to loving good, and be absolutely fair in all your dealings. If you do, it might be that the Lord will have mercy on at least a remnant of Israel.

"If you don't, there will be wailing and mourning around here that you can't imagine. Everybody in the city will join with the hired mourners in weeping, and even the usually happy vineyards and farms will be places of mourning once the Lord passes through our midst in judgment. Your nice preachers have been talking about the "Day of the Lord" as if they can hardly wait for it to come. They don't know what they are asking for!

"The Day of the Lord will be darkness, not light. Thinking that the Day of the Lord is going to take care of our troubles is like someone running from a lion right into the arms of a great bear, or finally running into a house to lean up against a wall to catch his breath—and have a snake bite him. You aren't going to get any help from the Lord you mock."

Maybe they said to each other, "I don't see why he says we aren't religious enough. Church attendance is better than it has been for years; the priests in our worship centers are working day and night trying to keep up with the sacrifices and offerings. We even have an orchestra to accompany the choir. Religion was never more popular."

"Let me see if I can clear up a point or two about that," Amos suggested. "You know what God thinks of your three festivals each year where the meaning is forgotten in the festivities and feasting? God hates them; I mean God despises them! You can offer up your burnt offerings and your cereal offerings all day but God will not accept them. Your so-called 'peace offerings' make the Lord sick. God doesn't want hymns and special music no matter how polished it is. All God wants is for us to do right in all our dealing all the time, like a stream that runs day and night. Doing justice constantly so that everybody can count on it, not just handing out food baskets on holidays, is real worship. The forty years Israel was in the wilderness the people weren't bringing God offerings and sacrifices. Now you have gone so far as to have floats in your religious parades with idols of Chaldean star gods!

"Well, the Lord says that you are going to be in another parade, one that takes you into exile where those false gods came from."

"Take it easy, Amos. That kind of talk makes people nervous," some of the leading citizens cautioned.

"Taking it easy is all you folks think about," Amos shot back. "Doesn't anybody see what incredibly tough times are coming to those who are taking their ease right now? The people who feel so secure in the big houses on the hill ought to feel most insecure. Haven't you seen what happened to some of the little kingdoms around us? Do you think it can't happen here?

"Just look at you! If you aren't sleeping in your ornate beds, or lounging on your plush couches, you are eating choice meats and drinking wine by the pitchers full. You spend a lot of time making sure you use the right bath oil and cosmetics, but you don't give a single thought to the coming ruin of the whole nation! You pampered rich people are going to be the first to be taken into exile and, believe me, there won't be any time for parties or recreation! God can't stand the pride and opulence of this city, and has sworn that it will soon be destroyed.

"How bad will it be? I'll tell you. Plague will wipe out everybody in a household, and when someone comes to burn the bodies, the lone survivor huddling in a corner will say 'Shhhh. Don't even mention the Lord's name. I don't want the Lord to finish me off too.' Big houses and small houses—they will all be destroyed. And all of it is coming because of the awful injustice of Israel.

"Horses don't run on rocks, and farmers don't try to plow the ocean with oxen. It is just as unnatural and ridiculous for you folks to try to live in a society that perverts justice. Even though you think that your little victories in taking Lodebar and Karnaim back from the Syrians show that Israel is well and strong, the Lord is going to send a real enemy against you and they will clean up on you from one end of the country to the other.

"Let me tell you, it isn't as if destroying this nation hasn't occurred to God before. I know of two times when the Lord considered it. Once God allowed me to see how locusts were gathering to swarm over the second crop of the year. They began to eat up all the green vegetation in sight. It was such a horrible sight that I begged God not to do it because Jacob is so small and weak as a nation. And the Lord decided not to do it.

"The second time I saw a scene of what was being planned that was even worse. God was going to burn everything up, even the ocean. And once again I broke down at the thought of it and prayed for our nation to be forgiven. Fortunately, again, the Lord relented.

"But the last time was different. Now God says that this judgment will come. I saw the Lord in the form of a carpenter standing beside a wall with a plumb line in hand. The plumb line would tell whether the wall was straight enough to stand. The carpenter-figure asked me what I saw.

"I see a plumb line," I replied.

"Yes, and I am setting a plumb line against the house of Israel. I can't let this kind of crooked and unsafe building go on any longer. It is all going to come crashing down, and the ruling house of Jeroboam is going to be killed with the sword."

"How long are we going to let this rabble-rouser get away with this?" the church leaders asked each other when they began to recoil from the visitor's speeches.

"It had better stop right now before he gets our people all stirred up," they all concurred with the leading priest of the Bethel sanctuary. So the priest, Amaziah, wasted no time in getting to King Jeroboam.

"Have you heard anything about this man, Amos, who has been preaching in the public squares?" Amaziah asked the king.

"Who hasn't?" the king answered.

"But have you heard the latest thing he is saying?"

The king's expression indicated that he knew he was going to hear it right now.

"It's terrible! Amos is saying that you are going to die by the sword, and that Israel is going to be taken away captive to foreign lands." After a pause for that to sink in, the priest asked, "Do you want me to run him out of town?"

With the king's assent, Amaziah went out to find Amos.

"You've made your last speech here, Mr. Prophet. I am ordering you in the name of the king to get out of our country right now. It's only five miles to the border and you can make it before sundown. You can preach all you want in Judah, and maybe they will let you live there. But don't ever again preach here in Bethel. This is the place of the king's sacred sanctuary. We don't allow such talk in our temple!"

"Don't call me a preacher," Amos shot back. "I'm not ordained clergy and my father isn't either. I work for a living taking care of sheep and pruning trees. But the Lord told me one day to leave my job and come up here to say these things in Israel. Now you are telling me not to tell the truth about what is going on here. Yet God is telling me to do it. So whom am I to obey?

"Well, I have a special word from the Lord to you, Amaziah. Your wife will be a prostitute in the city after your children are killed and all your property given away to others—because you are going to be dragged away as a captive to a pagan land."

The account doesn't say what happened then, but since the rest of the book reports other statements of Amos, we can assume that he wisely retreated across the border into Judah.

Chapter 8 opens with a scene familiar to artists who need a still-life model to study: a basket of summer fruit has caught Amos' attention. "This is the end of the line for that fruit," Amos thought. "So it is for the nation of Israel. It looks good now, but it will soon be gone. The beautiful temple music will turn to wailing, and in the city there will be dead silence as the bodies are piled up for burial."

The following few excerpts from his speeches give the gist of more comments he made to the soon-to-decay-summer-fruit society of Israel:

"Listen carefully, you callous rich people who take every unfair advantage of the poor who can't protect themselves, you merchants who can't wait for holy days to be over so you can get on with your money making. You cut the quality and quantity of your products and inflate the price. You cheat on the measurements and weights. You foreclose on a poor person for the price of a pair of sandals, and you add chaff and dirt to the wheat to cheat on your sales. This is what the Lord says to you:

"Don't think that I will forget what you are doing! Terrifying days are coming to this land because of you; they will come like a flood of the Nile, uprooting you and leaving you in the mud. It will be such a black day for you that the sun will go down at noon; your feasts will be times of mourning and your songs will all be sad funeral dirges. Your whole existence will be as sad as if you were mourning an only child."

That sad theme continues. "A famine is coming. This is worse than lack of bread and water; this is a famine of the human spirit. Nowhere will you find any strength from the word of the Lord—no matter where you go. Even your young men and women will die in spirit, cut apart from the inspiration of the Spirit. And all of those who look for life from other gods will simply die."

Even in church the relentless truth impressed itself on the mind of the shepherd-prophet. There he saw the Lord standing by the altar saying that everybody in the land was going to be battered and killed. Nobody will escape. Since God is bringing the punishment on them, they couldn't escape if they dug down to the underworld of Sheol or climbed up into heaven. There is no safe place on the top of Mt. Carmel or at the bottom of the ocean. Even the ones who are taken captive at first will be killed wherever they are taken.

If this was just an act of human enemies, there might be some escape. But the God who is complete Creator and Master of all the earth and everything in it is running this operation. The Lord is Creator of all peoples, the Ethiopians as well as the Hebrews. God not only brought Israel out of the bondage of Egypt one time; God also saved the Philistines from Caphtor, and the Syrians from Kir. The Lord cares for, and judges, them all. Israel isn't the only concern of God, so this sinful nation is expendable. The Lord is going to shake and sift this nation and none of the sinful people are going to fall through the sieve.

"Only a few good people will one day be brought back to begin to build again the house of David and restore the old kingdom. It's beyond the immediate future, and I can't see it, but the day will come, the Lord promises, when the land will be so productive that the harvesters will follow right along behind the sowers. The mountains will be dripping with juice. The ruined cities will be rebuilt, and the nation will be established once more by the Lord.

"This time it will be forever."

OBADIAH

Edict for Edom

Two verses shorter than *Haggai*, that makes this 21-verse "book" the shortest in the Old Testament. Only the Second and Third *Letters of John* in the New Testament are briefer.

Obadiah is short on quality too.

Written in those days following the final Babylonian conquest of Judah (this means we jumped forward another century and a half from *Amos*), *Obadiah* is a one-point outburst:

"Edom is going to catch it for kicking their neighbors in Judah when they were down."

*******   *******

"Edom, you think you are so strong, secure in your mountain stronghold. You are sitting there as smug as an eagle nesting on a mountaintop, but the Lord is going to pull you off your perch.

"Sometimes thieves will leave a few things they miss, and sometimes grape pickers miss a few. But your enemies will wipe you out completely. The funny thing is that the ones who will do you in are your former allies— the same dirty trick you pulled on Judah!

"You turned on your kinfolk in Judah and robbed and killed every bit as unmercifully as the conquering army of Babylon. Oh, you laughed at Judah then, but that was a bad mistake. Who's laughing now? You came into Jerusalem as it was being destroyed and looted it. You even caught some of our survivors and turned them over to the enemy. Now the Lord is giving you back what you have given. You, and the other nations around here, are going to vanish, and when you are all gone Mt. Zion will still be here as God's sacred place. The people of Judah will be back to possess this land which is still theirs by right. Just like the old story of Isaac's two sons, Jacob will again win out over Esau. Now no descendant of Edom (Esau) will survive.

"In the south the people of Jacob will occupy your country. In the west, the people of Judah will move down from the hills and take over the Philistine coast. Once again Jacob's people will occupy the former territory of Israel, then expand eastward through Gilead, and to the north and west to take over Phoenecia as well. The old kingdom of David will be reestablished, and the only king will be the Lord of Israel."

That's it.

JONAH

A Whale of a Story

The Jews are back. Under Ezra, Nehemiah and other leaders, they have established themselves in Jerusalem again. In Judah they hold the upper hand even though many other people live among them in the land, and the stricter Jews are making every effort to cut off relationships with them. The books of *Ezra* and *Nehemiah* state their position very plainly.

However, not everyone agreed. Some doubted that God wanted the Jews to forget that God cares for people of other nations as much as for the new Jewish state.

"If marriage to non-Jews is so detrimental to the well-being of Israel, how do you explain the entire royal line of David? His grandmother was a foreign woman from Moab." So the writer of *Ruth* points out with a wonderful love story.

The Isaiahs made the point clearly as well. "The foreigner who has joined the Lord does not have to say, 'The Lord will surely separate me from God's people. . .and the foreigners who. . .love the name of the Lord, everyone who keeps the sabbath and does not profane it, and holds fast to My covenant, these I will bring to My holy mountain. . .they will be accepted, etc.' " (Isaiah 56:3-8)

And somebody wrote this story about a Jew who was

so opposed to speaking to the people of Assyria that he actually refused to obey God—until he saw the light! In fact, call Jonah Ezra and imagine Ezra having the same commission, and you will catch the one big emphasis the little story is making.

Better still, call Jonah by your name and read it. Instead of preaching to Ninevah, substitute the one job you would least like for God to call you to do.

* * * * * * *

He sat straight up in bed, eyes wide open.

"What did You say, Lord?"

"I said that I want you to go on a preaching mission to Ninevah and try to get them to repent and turn to Me."

"That's what I thought You said."

Morning light had barely broken the dark veil of the eastern sky when Jonah was packing his bag. When the Lord said "Go," here was a person who would hit the road. But we only get past two verses before we find a surprise ending to the story already. Jonah was going, but he was heading in the opposite direction!

As long as God stayed sensible, Jonah would do what God requested. But, obviously, the strain of taking care of all creation had finally gotten to the Lord and somehow a cog had slipped. The best thing to do was to clear out of the jurisdiction of the God of Israel. So Jonah headed for the coast.

"I've heard that Tarshish is at the other end of the Great Sea," Jonah said to himself. "Nobody there has ever heard of our God. I'm going there until this confusion in God's mind passes."

The next morning found Jonah on the dock.

"Ticket for one to Tarshish—one way," he was saying. The fare paid, he boarded the vessel and found his way down to his bunk in the lower deck. He was watching closely when the lines were cast off and the ship pulled away from its mooring. Only then did he breathe a sigh of relief. So far, so good.

Not so fast, Jonah.

The rising wind and the crashing waves seemed to be just another Mediterannean storm until their fury stirred up the latent storm in Jonah's conscience.

"Lord, You aren't behind this, are You?"

Everybody else was sure that some god was getting personal about it. Each one of them probably suspected secretly that it was his own sin which was causing the dangerous situation. So they got busy with their prayers of repentance, and at the same time, in order to lighten the boat, they were throwing overboard everything that was loose.

The captain was looking for expendable material down in the hold when he came across Jonah who was trying to sleep as if nothing unusual was happening.

"Hey you! What are you doing down here?" the captain jabbed Jonah verbally. "Get up and call on your god. We need all the help we can get."

The more they prayed and worried, the worse the storm became. So if prayer won't work, try chance. It wasn't hard to find a pair of dice among sailors. They rolled the dice to see whose number would turn up.

"Snake eyes!" they said. "That's you, Jonah. You want to tell us all about it? Who are you anyway? Where do you come from? What is your occupation?"

"I'm a Hebrew," Jonah choked out. "And I worship the One God Who made the earth and the sea."

"Oh, my (gosh)" they muttered as they drew back from him. "Then it must be you. What have you done to bring this on us? We are going to have to do something to quiet this sea before our ship is smashed to pieces!"

Now Jonah is resigned to his fate. "You'd better throw me overboard. That's the only way to stop this storm my God has sent."

(He may be running from God, but a man who is willing to sacrifice himself for the safety of other people can't be as far from God as he had thought.)

"You may be right," one of the men replied, "but, boys, let's give it one more try with the oars to get to shore." Tired and frightened as they were, they pulled on the oars until they couldn't muster any more strength. Every wave pushed them farther from safety. So, exhausted, they knew they had to do it.

"God, forgive us, but we know we have to give up Jonah in order to get You to spare our own lives."

Over the side he went, hardly making a splash in the giant swell that almost tossed the ship onto its side— one last great shuddering of the sea before the storm began to subside. What nobody saw was the mammoth fish that turned away from the side of the ship just after Jonah disappeared beneath the surface.

Jonah never saw it either, because it was very dark on the inside of that fish. As unbelievable as it may be, Jonah had been swallowed whole by this denizen of the deep.

Night and day were not to be distinguished in the fish's interior, but above the ocean's surface three days and nights passed before Jonah's new situation was to change.

"I wanted to get away from You, Lord, and here I am at the bottom of the sea. I can't go any farther. Still, I can't seem to escape Your Presence. Even though I may not ever again set foot in the holy temple of Jerusalem, I know now that You can hear my prayer here as well as there."

And right there, in the belly of a fish in the bottom

of the sea, Jonah, the man who had said "No" to God now said "Yes."

"I don't know what use I can be now, but I'm Yours to command," Jonah said in finishing his prayer. He was soon to discover that though his situation had changed, God's long-run plan for him had not changed.

"Swim east until you beach yourself, and spit out this repentant preacher you are carrying," the Lord told the fish. This time Jonah was headed in the right direction.

"Keep moving, Jonah," the Lord said, "and I will tell you what to say when you get to Ninevah."

"Yes, Lord. It's good to see some daylight in my life again."

Everybody had heard about the great capital of the Assyrian world, but Jonah was not prepared for this Los Angeles of the Near East.

"It would take three days to walk across this city," he said in amazement when he topped a rise just west of town and saw it spreading along the valley of the Tigris River. "I'll just start into it, I guess, and keep going until the Lord stops me." And just before suppertime, right at rush hour for the traffic of people getting off work, it happened. He found himself standing on a street corner and saying at the top of his voice: "Forty days is all you have. Then this big city will be overthrown!"

He couldn't believe what happened next. Traffic stopped. People crowded around him to say "Overthrown? What do you mean? Who's going to do it? What are you talking about?"

He wasn't sure later what all he said. The Lord seemed to give him words as he told them about the God of all nations who did not want to see them destroyed by their own wickedness. All over the city the word spread. How could he have known that the most wicked city in the world was ready to change its heart and ways? This was God's doing, and he wasn't sure he liked it. He had come to prophesy their immediate doom, which he and most of the world would rejoice to see. But here they were proclaiming fasts, praying for forgiveness, asking God to save them!

Even the king joined the prayer meeting, leaving his royal robes for the sackcloth and ashes of a religious penitent. Everywhere they were announcing his imperial decree that every person, even the animals, must join in a whole day of fasting and prayer for God's guidance so that they could put aside all the wickedness and violence that had marked their life together.

"If we only have forty days then we had better get busy making the changes God requires," the king said.

They didn't use the same name for God that Jonah used, nor did they speak the same language. They weren't in the temple of Jerusalem, and they had never read the law of Moses. But God, Who looks on the heart, understood their sincerity and accepted their offering of themselves. God forgave, and called off the plan to destroy the city.

Everybody was happy except Jonah.

"I knew it. I just knew it! Something told me that if I followed Your orders and came here to preach that Your love and mercy would win out over Your plans for punishment. That's why I tried to get away to Tarshish so You couldn't get me mixed up with these heathen gentiles. I'd rather die than defile myself any further with these contacts."

"O come on now, Jonah, do you think it is right that you should feel this way?" The Lord could have added, "You know that you couldn't escape your conscience even in the belly of the fish. What makes you think you can sit down now under a lean-to here on this hill east of Ninevah and forget all I have said through My best prophets?" But instead, the Lord had a fast-growing plant rise behind him to shield him from the heat of the sun while Jonah sat there hoping to see God carry out the original plan of destruction. Jonah even remembered to say, "Thank you, Lord, for the shade."

The next day dawned and Jonah planned to rest another day waiting for the catastrophe to happen. So pleased was he with his thoughts of vengeance that he didn't even notice the worm that was cutting down the stalk of his shade plant. As soon as the hot sun and the dry wind off the desert hit it, the plant withered and, before he knew it, Jonah was a candidate for sunstroke.

"I can't stand any more of this, Lord. I'd be better off dead. Why did this plant have to wither when I need it so much? Don't You care? I was really fond of that plant," Jonah added wistfully.

"Well, I'm glad to see you can have pity on something," the Lord replied with a touch of sarcasm. "You are fond of a plant which grew up overnight with no effort or care from you at all, a plant you saw for only one day. Should I not have any pity for this great city where a hundred and twenty thousand innocent pre-school children live?"

Jonah doesn't make any reply. The author doesn't add anything else. It's up to the reader to say: "Of course!"

Now, should our own non-Jewish friends and family members here in Judah be forced out of our homes and denied access to the temple when God cares even for the worst enemies Israel ever knew?

Jonah is a fish story where the fish got away, but the man who came home with the story couldn't!

MICAH

Collision Course

They made a great one-two punch, Isaiah and Micah, with Micah following up the lead of Isaiah in Judah the way Hosea complemented the preaching of Amos in Israel.

Isaiah was the big-city boy, born and raised in the top society of Jerusalem. Micah was a small-town or country boy, from Moresheth, twenty or so miles southwest of Jerusalem on the road to Gath in Philistia. But he was no country bumpkin. He knew what was going on in the capital city and he probably did most of his preaching there. Among other things, rich landowners in the city needed to hear what God thought of their continuing takeover of small family farms and ranches.

The first three chapters are a sermon that pretty well wraps up what they heard him say.

"Now hear this, all of you! If you think the Lord is confined to the holy temple, you are mistaken. God is moving in judgment on this whole land. Like a volcanic eruption that melts the solid mountains like water, the fire of God's judgment will be poured out on the people of Jacob.

" 'Not Samaria; not Jerusalem!' you say. Listen, Samaria will be nothing but a heap of stones in the open country; only the foundations of buildings will be left to mark where the city was. All those ornate places of worship will be completely destroyed, the idols and images smashed and burned. Like hired prostitutes, those idols that came in from foreign lands (notably Assyria) will be returned.

"I will be the first to cry over Samaria's destruction, sympathizing with those who go into exile stripped naked. (Isaiah actually acted out the stripped and naked object lesson for three years.) I will make as much sorrowful noise mourning as the jackals and ostriches, but our mourning should not be just for Samaria. The same incurable disease has entered the gates of Jerusalem!

"This is bad, bad news for everybody. Pardon the puns, but this shouldn't be told in Gath (pun on the word 'tell'). In Bethleaphrah (dust town) roll yourselves in the dust; people of Shaphir (like Fairview), you will make a pretty sight being led away naked; and the inhabitants of Zaanan (meek, or sheep) had better hide in town."

His puns on Bethezel and Maroth we don't get—who said they were the lowest forms of humor? —but Lachish, among the first of Solomon's "chariot cities" is a symbol to Micah of the trust in military might that began the ruin of Israel and Judah. Now military might will destroy it. And the people of the prophet's own home town, Moresheth, should pass out going-away presents. "Achzib sounds like our word for 'deceit,' doesn't it? Well, the big houses there will be a deceitful thing to the leaders of Judah. You've seen conquerors before, Mareshah; now another one is coming. The glory of Israel will end up back in the caves of Adullam where David had to hide.

"Go ahead, all of you, and shave your heads. Make yourselves as bald as buzzards, because you and your children are going bald-headed into exile."

(Micah had named the towns of the western foothills of Judah, all of which would be in the line of invasion if Sargon, emperor of Assyria, came to attack Jerusalem, moving his forces from the coast where he had just put down an uprising in Gaza.)

"Why is all this coming? Because rich people lie awake at night thinking up new ways to oppress the poor people. The next day they put their evil schemes into practice. They covet the fields and houses of small farmers so they take them, robbing people of all their inheritance. That's why God is bringing punishment they cannot escape. All this ill-gotten wealth will be torn from them, and there will not even be any male descendants left to take part in the assembly of the Lord.

"I know you don't like to hear these things! You keep saying 'don't mix religion with politics. Stick to the spiritual message!' Are you saying that God is not concerned about these matters? Any just person who is trying to do right would see that these words are true and must be spoken. It has to be pointed out that the true enemies of Judah are those who exploit the people. That is you who dispossess women and children from their houses, leaving them no place to go. You are worse than an enemy who would attack these peaceful citizens in war.

"What kind of preaching do you want to hear? Find some windbag who spouts a lot of hot air, and can tell you how to mix cocktails for the social hour! That's the only kind of preacher for you. Such a preacher can reassure you that all of you will be gathered by the Lord into a nice sheepfold in the midst of danger. Then the Lord will open a way for everyone to march safely through the enemy lines, with the king striding in front, following the Lord Who leads in glory.

"Rubbish! Hear this real word from the Lord, you ruling people of Israel: Aren't you charged with setting up a rule of justice? Yet you hate the good and love the evil. Instead of protecting the people, you almost literally eat them up and skin them alive. When your time comes to be chopped up, you will cry to the Lord, but there is no way God will help you.

"Where have the prophets and preachers stood in these days? They have been preaching the nice 'spiritual' sermons about peace and comfort when the people don't have bread to eat. The poor people are not putting bread in their mouths, so these false prophets speak out on behalf of those who pay them. Blind as they are, darkness will be all they will ever know. When the day of truth comes they will be seen for the cheap imitations of prophets that they are. But, I, for one, am moved only by the Spirit of the Lord, and I am denouncing this sin of Israel and Judah with all my might.

"So, listen once again, you leading citizens, you who hate justice and pervert the law, you who try to build our nation on violence and oppression. The courts give judgments for bribes; the priests teach whatever the contributors want to hear, and the prophets conjure up visions to get money, not the will of God. And yet you all stand and sing 'Leaning On The Lord,' and think that the Lord is with you and no evil will ever come to you!

"It's because of you that Jerusalem is going to be bare as a plowed field, and the only thing on Mount Zion will be trees and brush."

Obviously, chapter 4 does not follow the line of thought that marked all of Micah's sermon in the first three chapters. Micah may have said what follows in chapters 4 and 5, but in a different setting and time. More likely, this writing is added from a date after the fall of Jerusalem to the Babylonians. Since the last thing mentioned in Micah's speech was the "mountains of the house of the Lord," this passage, also found in *Isaiah* 2:2-5, was inserted here:

"It shall come to pass someday that the mountain of the

house of the Lord shall be raised up above all other holy places. People of all nations will come to it, saying to each other 'Let's go to the temple on the mountain of the Lord so that we can learn the ways of the Lord of Israel.' The true word of the Lord will spread out from Jerusalem to cover the world until it becomes the measure by which all nations make their judgments. They will all beat their swords into plowshares, and their spears into pruning hooks. No nation will go to war against another nation; people won't even learn about war anymore. Every person will be perfectly safe on his/her own property, and nobody will have any cause to fear anyone else. This is God's own promise.

"Now (verse 5) everyone follows his or her own god, but we will follow the Lord God forever.

"Finally the day will come when all the abused people, the crippled, the exiles who were driven off into captivity, all the cast-offs, will be brought back by the Lord to Mount Zion. And they will be welded into a strong nation again. Remember that in these days when you are without leadership that can give you good counsel. Now you are hurting like a woman in labor; now you will be forced into exile, but in Babylon the Lord will rescue you and redeem you from your enemies.

"Now other nations plot their attack on Zion, but they don't know that God is drawing them here like sheaves of wheat for threshing. Yet there will come that time when you will stamp all over them; you will beat them to pieces and take all their wealth and offer it to the Lord.

"Now you are hemmed in and humiliated as the conquerors make sport of striking your king. But there will come a day when once again from little Bethlehem will come a ruler from the line of David. The travail through which you are now going is a necessary prelude to his coming. Then when he comes in the strength of the Lord he will feed the flock of Israel as the shepherd-king long ago. That great kingdom of David will be restored.

"When the seven shepherd brothers of David join with the king they form a band as eight princes who shall be strong enough to ward off any enemies, even Assyria. They will conquer, and the remnant of Judah will be like a lion among sheep. The renewed Israel will be powerful enough to put down all their former enemies.

" 'Then,' the Lord says, 'you won't need military might anymore. War horses, chariots, fortresses will all be gone. And with them all the pagan practices that have been part of the cult worship will go too. Those stupid images and idols you made with your own hands will be thrown away. The pillars which reminded you of false gods, and all those objects connected with the Canaanite fertility goddess, will be destroyed. I hate them.' (Verse 14 of chapter 5 probably should read "and destroy your idols" instead of "cities.")

" 'Let's get down to cases,' chapter 6 opens with the Lord's challenge. 'You tell these mountains around here what you have against Me, and I will tell My side of the story. I brought you out of the bondage of Egypt and gave you Moses, Aaron and Miriam to lead you. Think back on your history of how I brought you into the Promised Land. Have you forgotten?' "

Since the last two chapters seem to be written as liturgy for a worship service, the congregation now responds:

"With what shall I come before the Lord, and bow myself before God?

"Shall I come before God only with burnt offerings of choicest year-old calves?

"Would God be pleased with thousands of rams and ten thousand rivers of oil?

"Shall I offer my first-born child to be devoted to the

Lord as a way of making up for my own sin?

"No. God has shown us what is good, and what is required of us: 'do justice, love kindness, and walk humbly with the Lord!'

(There it is, a statement of God's preference that has never been surpassed!)

"If that is what God requires," the leader picks up, "then look how far we have fallen. Our treasuries are full of ill-gotten gains. Merchants have been shortchanging customers. Scales have been falsified; business practices are as dishonest as can be. Rich people use force against the poor; people would rather tell lies than the truth. Deceit has displaced trust.

"That's why God has begun to punish us. Even though we have plenty to eat, our spiritual hunger cannot be satisfied. So our material stores won't do us any good. All this stuff we are stockpiling will be destroyed or taken away. What we are planting we will never get to harvest for ourselves. We will be crushing olives, but we will never get the oil. We will be treading grapes, but the wine won't be for us. Destruction is coming to us because we have followed King Omri and King Ahab in false religion. Now we are going to be so wiped out that everyone will hiss when our name is mentioned.

"We have it coming too. You would really have to search to find a godly person in this country. Everyone is looking for ways to hurt or trick other H.B.s. They are all past masters at doing evil, and they seem to be proud of it. Judges and government officials actually ask for bribes; every person is busy weaving his or her part of the evil tapestry. The best people are like briars, and all together they are like a hedge of thorns. Now, with their day of punishment coming, they are all confused because there is no one anyone can trust. You can't tell anything in confidence to your best friend, not even to your wife or husband. Sons treat their own fathers with contempt, and daughters turn against their mothers. Your enemies may be right in your own house.

"Only God can be trusted, so I am putting all my faith in the Lord. I will wait for God to act. My enemies may put me down, but I will rise again. Even in the darkness my Lord will be a light for me. My punishment is deserved, so I will take it until the Lord chooses to deliver me. Then the people who taunt me saying 'Where is the Lord your God?' will know, and it will be their turn to be trampled in the mud."

Now the focus of attention swings back from the act of confession and the affirmation of faith in God to another look at the promised future.

"Yes, the day for rebuilding is coming. The old boundaries will be extended again from Egypt on the south to the Euphrates River on the northeast, from the sea on the west to the mountains of the interior. Much of the rest of the earth will be desolate because of what the people have been doing. But God will be the shepherd of this special flock, and just like the good old days when God brought us out of the land of Egypt we will see marvelous things. When the other nations see it, they will come crawling like snakes to beg pardon from our God.

"Lord, there isn't anything or anybody to compare with You! You don't keep Your anger forever, but You forgive us and You will have compassion on us again. We know that. You will cast our sins and guilt into the sea, and You will still make good the promise You made to Abraham and all our fathers and mothers in the old days. All we can do now is wait for that."

NAHUM

Last Rites!

Nahum led the cheers for the fall of Ninevah, just as Obadiah exulted over the destruction of Edom a few years later. Since Edom was much smaller than great Assyria, of which Ninevah was the capital and nerve center, Obadiah didn't take quite as many lines to do it.

For many generations the people of Israel and Judah had joined their prayers for the destruction of Assyria to those of the other little nations of the Middle East. Probably no empire has ever been as heavy-handed and mean as Assyria. So when that empire began to crack, and the fall of the capital was imminent, a man of Judah we know only by name, Nahum, spoke out enthusiastically:

"We told you so! The Lord God may take a long time to get around to it, but sooner or later the guilty will be punished!

"The Lord walks in tornados and storms, stirring up clouds like dust from the feet, drying up rivers and seas and wooded mountains, and shaking the earth at will. Who thought they could stand against God's anger when divine wrath is poured out?

"Of course, for those who take refuge in our God, the Lord is good, giving strength in their day of trouble. But the enemies of the Lord will be burned up like dry stubble or thorns. Now the Lord is saying to us: 'I afflicted you with tough punishment, but now I am going to let up on you. Your enemies are going to be cut off, and your bonds of slavery will be broken.'

"'This is what God is saying to Ninevah: 'You've had it. All of your vile images and idols will be destroyed, and you along with them!'

"And to Judah: 'The feet of the messenger with good tidings is already on the way. Renew your vows and keep your religious observances because the wicked oppressors will never stop you again.' "

Now the prophet-crier directs his judgment toward Ninevah.

"Get ready for the attack. Gather all your forces for the defense of your city. But I can already see how the battle will go. The big red army is charging in, chariots flashing in the sun, cavalry units racing back and forth across the city squares as the outer barriers fall. A second line of defense is set up along an inner wall; the defenders raise their shields; officers are uncertain what to do; the river gates are forced open and the palace is overrun; the queen is stripped and carried off while all her servant girls cry and wail. Everything is panic, and the people of the city stream out of Ninevah like water from a broken dike.

"I can hear the orders, 'Back, back, turn to fight!' but the retreat is now a complete rout. All resistance is over, and the plundering of the city has begun. Every valuable item and every precious treasure is being found and taken. Everywhere I look the destruction is mounting, with the people of Ninevah cowering in fear and anguish!

"Oh no! This can't be the great lion's den, can it? Surely this isn't the fearful place to which he dragged his prey to be torn apart by the young lions! What happened? The lion is trembling now.

" 'The sword is cutting down your young lions,' says the Lord of hosts. 'No longer will they prey on the people of the earth. Your chariots will burn in smoke and flame.'

"Plunder, plunder this bloody city!

"Whips cracking, wheels rumbling, horses galloping, chariots lunging, horsemen charging, swords flashing, spears glittering. . .heaps of corpses, piles of dead bodies, death and dying everywhere! So death comes to the deadly deceitful harlot who led so many people astray, who betrayed so many nations. Now you are shamed in the sight of all the nations. They look on your nakedness with all your splendor torn from you, and they throw garbage at you, and they spit with contempt. . .the beautiful city so wasted away!

"Who is there to mourn for you now, Ninevah?

"Remember Thebes which thought itself secure far up the Nile, with allies all around to bolster the defense of Egypt? Yet you destroyed her, murdering little children, leading her citizens away in chains to captivity (the Assyrian victory under Ashurbanipal in 663 B.C.). Now it is your turn to reel like a drunken, dazed coward looking for a place to hide. All your fortresses are falling like ripe figs when the tree is shaken; the gates are all wide open to your enemies; fire has devoured your barriers, and your troops are like unarmed women.

"Too late to lay in water and supplies for a seige, or to build up your defenses with more brick! The fire and sword are cutting you down already. Your soldiers and merchants have swarmed over the earth like locusts and grasshoppers; they were everywhere. But now, suddenly, they are gone like the swarm at sunrise, and nobody knows where they are.

"O mighty king of Assyria, your subjects are gone, all of them—your shepherds, your nobles, your people all gone. It's all over for you; this wound is fatal. Is that the clapping of hands we hear? Yes, the applause is growing everywhere, because there is no place where your terror was not known.

"This celebration is for your fall!"

HABAKKUK

The Lord's Game Plan

"Lord, how long am I going to keep crying for help without getting any answer? I know You can see the violence and injustice that is going on around here, but I can't see that You are doing anything about it. The wicked people go on perverting justice and taking advantage of the innocent." (1:2-4)

That's a prophet named Habakkuk praying in the time of Jeremiah, when Jehoiakim had abandoned the reform program of his father, Josiah. And the Lord, Who could see that Jehoiakim's new alliance with Egypt would bring the Babylonians back, put this answer in Habakkuk's mind:

"I am taking care of the local situation even if you can't see anything happening yet. I am calling the Babylonians in again. They are good at trampling down other nations. In fact, they will swarm all over this place like a pack of leopards or wolves. Their cavalry units won't waste any time getting here, and when they get here they will sweep everything clean. They'll laugh at these fortresses, make a sport of capturing kings, and carry off captives in droves. These guys are wicked and tough; they play by their own rules." (1:5-11)

"But, Lord," Habakkuk comes back, "why do You pick them to chastise us? You are too pure to look on evil; that's why You must punish Judah. But why do You let people that are more wicked than we are swallow us up? That's hard for me to understand. These people are like fishermen, and all the rest of the people of the world are like fish caught by their hooks or nets. They drag us in and then worship their own nets and seines because they think they are able to do all this by their own might. How long are You going to let them keep throwing their nets over other nations to kill them? I will stay here at my station in the temple until I can get an answer to that." (1:12-2:1)

"Well, take that vision," the Lord replied, "and write it on stone tablets in big plain letters: 'The Lord is sending the Babylonians to destroy Judah!' It may take a little time for that to happen, but it surely will happen in the end. And when it comes, the righteous person will still have life in its truest sense, but the unrighteous person will have nothing to cling to. Wine, wealth, and arrogant power can never assure that life- support. (2:2-5a) That same thing applies to the king of Babylon who is gobbling up all the nations." (2:5b)

"That's certainly true," Habakkuk agrees. "Here at home the tyrant who is amassing wealth that is not his own, taking 'pledges' like a pawn broker for loans and services from people who can't make the payments, will find that the people turn on him finally. On the world scale it will happen too. The remnants of the plundered people of the nations will some day rise to plunder great Babylon.

"You can't set yourself on a perch high enough, Jehoia-kim, to be safe from harm. By acting so shamefully, you are bringing judgment on your own life. The beams and stones of this palace you have built by taxing your poor people cry out against you. (2:6-11)

"Neither will the king of Babylon who builds his city on the blood of captive laborers. All that work will perish in fire, but finally the whole earth will be filled with the knowledge of the glory of God as the waters cover the sea. (2:12-14) But you, Jehoiakim, who have gotten your kicks out of seeing your neighbors in misery, like a drug pusher who gets people drunk so he can laugh at their shame, your cup will be filled with contempt, not glory. The Lord will make you drink of the cup of judgment, and you will stagger in your shame. The same destruction that has come to Lebanon is coming to you and to all the cities and people of your kingdom." (2:13-17)

And while we are at it, some editor said later, let's throw in a little sarcasm about idol-making, the way Isaiah did.

"Isn't it strange how a workman shapes up an idol for himself and then trusts in it as if it were god? There it sits, either stone or wood overlaid with gold and silver. It is not alive, and never was, but he asks the dumb idol to speak and give him some revelation about life.

"No, only the Lord Who is in the holy temple is alive, and all the earth should keep reverent silence before the one true God!" (2:18-20)

"There is nothing left to do but pray for our God's will to be done," Habakkuk concludes in chapter 3.

"O Lord, I have heard of so many things You have done, and I have great respect for Your work. Now, in our days, do it again: show us Your mercy.

"You came to us first from Sinai, with glory covering the heavens, and the earth filled with Your praise. Your brightness was like the flashing light of the sun, and Your wrath created pestilence and plague. Your judgment measured the earth, shaking the mountains and the nations. Cush and Midian and the other nations trembled before You. Nothing, not even the rivers or oceans could stand before You. Like a mighty warrior whose arrows and spear strike down all opposition, You created the earth and sea, the sun and moon and everything there is. And when You moved against the nations which opposed Your anointed people, You crushed them all. Whenever an enemy came to destroy our nation, You trampled that puny force with Your might.

"When I consider all this, I tremble and grow faint, and I realize I have no strength on my own. I must wait patiently for the present invaders to be overthrown as well. Even when the fig tree does not blossom, and no fruit grows on the vine; even when the olive trees fail to produce and the fields are barren; even when all the flocks are gone, I will still trust You to be our final salvation. You, O God, are my strength. You make my feet as sure as the feet of the hind which tracks safely across steep places."

This is about as good a note as any for an ending.

ZEPHANIAH

Your Time is Coming

Not all the sons of kings become kings themselves. Kings had a lot of children who didn't make it, but King Hezekiah (the by-and-large good king Isaiah visited in the hospital) had a great, great-grandson who was a prophet in the early days of another reformer king named Josiah. And young Zephaniah left his name on a little book in our *Bible*.

The first two verses of his word from the Lord sound as if they might have been intended for the sixth chapter of *Genesis* when the Lord was talking to Noah. "I'm going to wipe out everything and everybody," the word came. But by verse four it is apparent that the Lord's anger is directed mainly against the Hebrew part of the earth.

"It's Judah I'm going to get," the Lord says, "especially the worshippers of Baal, and those who bow down on rooftops before the sun, moon and stars as if they were gods. I'll also get those who bow down to Me, but who still swear by the Babylonia god, Milcom. Nobody really seeks My opinion any more."

"I'm telling you all," Zephaniah spoke out, "our best bet is to be silent before the Lord God. That 'Day of the Lord' is at hand. The Lord has set a time for inspection of what is going on here. The officials, even the king's sons, who dress up in foreign fashions, and the whole bunch that enters the king's house to carry on dishonest business, will be caught and punished.

"On that day there will be weeping and wailing all over town; there will be no 'business as usual.' The Lord will search all the dark nooks and crannies with a lamp to find and punish the people who drink even the dregs of the wine while they say 'The Lord won't do anything about it, neither good nor bad.' Well, all their goods will be plundered and their houses destroyed. As Amos said, 'They will build houses but they won't get to live in them; they will plant vineyards but they won't get to drink wine from them.'

"The great day of the Lord's judgment is near, and it will be a bitter one:

distress and anguish...
ruin and devastation...
darkness and gloom...
clouds and thick darkness...
trumpet blast and battle cry...

Sinners will walk like the blind, blood pouring out on the ground, and not all their silver and gold will be able to save them. All the earth will feel God's wrath; none will escape judgment.

"Now is the time to call a solemn national assembly," the prophet advises, "so this shameless nation can repent before you are all driven away like chaff in the wind. Let all the humble people of the land, those who try to obey the Lord's commands and do right, pray to the Lord to hide them on that Day. Everybody else is in for a rough time. Gaza, Ashkelon, Ashdod and Ekron, and all the inhabitants of the coastlands will be rooted up. Canaan will be destroyed. All Philistia will be grazing ground for the remnant of Judah someday, with sheep and cattle bedding down in the remains of the buildings.

"Moab and Ammon who are taking advantage of Judah's weakness now will feel God's destruction as well. Those countries will be like Sodom and Gomorrah, briar fields and salt pits, and what is left of them will be taken over by the survivors of Judah. God's judgment is against them too, and will continue until all the little gods of all the nations bow down to acknowledge the Lord.

"One by one they will all fall: Ethiopia to the south and Assyria to the north. Great Ninevah will be a desolate place where cattle bed down, a capital ruled by vultures and hedgehogs, with owls hooting in the palace windows and crows croaking on the thresholds. This is the proud city that thought it would be No. 1 forever. What a desolation it has become!

"And speaking of cities that are going to feel God's wrath," Zephaniah continues in chapter 3, "what about Jerusalem?" Jerusalem has not listened to any good advice. She will not accept any correction, and she will not trust the Lord her God."

(We should know by now that when a prophet takes the time to spell out the disaster that is coming to the other nations around Judah he is going to get around to his own nation sooner or later. After all, these are the people to whom he is preaching.)

"The officials and judges right here at home are like lions or wolves preying on the very people they are supposed to protect. The prophets are undisciplined, faithless people, and the priests actually lead in profaning sacred services and the law of God. God is still here showing justice and mercy, but the wicked people here show no shame whatsoever. So God is wondering what to do next.

"The Lord has laid waste to nations all around. You can't find an inhabitant in some of them anymore, and you'd think that Jerusalem would take notice and shape up. But the people here only seem more determined to be corrupt. So, just wait; your time is coming. The judgment of the Lord upon all the nations will consume Judah as well.

"Someday the Lord will have everybody on earth speaking one language (Hebrew?), so that everyone will be able to worship and serve the God of Israel. From the ends of the earth, even from beyond Ethiopia in distant Africa, they will bring offerings. Part of the preparation for that day will be the removal from your midst of the arrogant and haughty leaders, so that you won't be ashamed of their actions on the holy mountain. The people God will leave here will be humble and willing to seek refuge in the Lord. They will be truthful, gentle, right-living people who will not be afraid of anyone because they trust God."

All of which calls for a little song of celebration as the last six verses of the book.

"Lift your heart in song, Jerusalem!
Hard times are over; your enemies downed.
The Lord is the King of Israel again,
Fear vanishes where God is crowned.

"In love the Lord renews you now;
Dry every tear and join the song.
Outcast, lame and blind shall lead
The victory march of Judah's throng.

"From shame to praise, the nations change
Their estimate of Your worth. From last to first,
Your rise proclaims 'The Lord rules heaven and
    earth!' ''

HAGGAI

Top Priority

"I think we ought to be ashamed," Haggai said one day.

"Ashamed of what?" some of the people asked as they sat in a town meeting of the Jews who had returned from Babylon to the ruins of Jerusalem almost twenty years before.

"Ashamed that we have built nice houses for ourselves, but haven't even started to build the House of the Lord. And that's what we said we were coming back to do!"

"That sounds good if you say it quick," one man remarked. "But we can hardly scratch out a living for ourselves, and we are working night and day. We can't get any good crops to grow; we don't have enough clothing to keep warm in the winter; and any money we earn goes in payments and taxes as if we were putting our money into a bag that had holes in it. Looks like temple building is going to have to wait a while 'till we get straightened out."

"You just made my speech for me," Haggai came back. "Think about what you just said. The Lord is saying that you aren't going to have any divine favor until you build the temple again. Who do you think is withholding the rain and making it so hard on us? Put God first and then you will prosper too."

"It makes sense," Zerubbabel, the governor appointed by King Cyrus of Persia, said.

"It may be just the project we need to pull us together and raise our spirit," agreed Joshua, the high priest. Together they got the whole assembly enthusiastic enough to accept Haggai's challenge. Somebody even marked the day on the calendar when the work crew showed up to begin: the 24th day of the 6th month of the 2nd year of the reign of Darius the king. However, a month later they still didn't have much to show for their labor, and some were already getting discouraged.

"It's time for another pep talk," the Lord said to Haggai. So the prophet got the leaders and the people together again and asked if there were any people among them who remembered the old temple of Solomon. "I know this building doesn't look like much compared to the great temple we used to have, but at least it is ours, and the Lord is calling us to keep working on it. It may not seem so great to us now, but don't you see how the Lord will use it to fulfill the promise that all nations will come to honor and praise God here?

"We don't have to worry about getting silver and gold to make it beautiful. All silver and gold belongs to God, and God will see that this House will be more glorious than the old temple before all is said and done."

Another two months passed and Haggai spurred them along with a question that was intended to show the priests and people how important it was to get the temple finished and the pure religious sacrifices and ordinances going again.

"What if someone carried something that was holy or sacred in a pocket and that pocket touched bread or any other food—does that make the food holy?"

The priests answered, "No. Holiness isn't contagious."

"But what if someone who is unclean because he or she touched a dead body touches some food article—does the food become unclean?"

"Yes," they told him, "because filth, or disease, or sin is contagious."

"Well, that's just the way it is with these people," the prophet reasoned. "They live unclean lives, so when they come to worship their gifts and sacrifices are offered with unclean hands. Now think again about how you got along before the temple building began. Everything you touched turned up sour or short. Blight, mildew, bad weather, combined to ruin your crops and frustrate your work. Right? But from the day you started to build the House of the Lord, good things have happened. Crops are good, orchards are producing, and everything is looking up. God is surely blessing this project."

Carried away with the idea of God's favor now being shown again to the little Judah community, Haggai moved on to tell the governor, Zerubbabel, that the time was coming soon when the Lord would upset all the nations so that they would destroy themselves in civil war. Judah would be left as signet ring of the Lord, and Zerubabbel would be the jewel at the top of the ring. Presumably, he would be king, restoring the line of David.

Zerubbabel didn't get to be king. In fact, we never hear of him again. But the tendency on the part of Jewish thinkers to expect a Messiah to come as God's anointed leader continued to grow after Haggai's day. As far as they could see, the only possible source of new freedom and independence was God.

They were right, weren't they?

ZECHARIAH

Trust God and Keep Working

Haggai wasn't alone.

His buddy, Zechariah, was right there with him, urging the people to get going with the temple-building business. Zechariah had even more to say about how the new temple would fit into God's overall plans.

"I hope you aren't going to be like your parents and ancestors," he announced one day. "The Lord told them repeatedly through the prophets that if they would come back from their evil ways that God would return to them. They wouldn't listen. We know what happened to them. Let's not make that same mistake in our day!"

Three months later he had a vision he just had to tell everybody about.

"I saw a man riding a red horse. He was standing in a grove of myrtle trees, and behind him were red, white, and sorrel horses. I asked an angel (I had to ask somebody), 'what is all this?'

"He will tell you," the angel said, nodding toward the rider. And the rider spoke up: 'We have been out patrolling the earth for the Lord.' And then to the angel he added, 'everything on earth seems to be at rest.'

"At that, the angel looked up and said, 'Lord, how long will You have no mercy on Judah? It's been seventy years now.'

"The Lord answered the angel, and the angel turned back to me to say 'The Lord really cares for Jerusalem and Mt. Zion. You can tell your people that. And you can also tell the big nations that are on top now that they overdid the punishment which God intended for Judah. Now that the temple is being rebuilt the Lord intends to return to it. From there Jerusalem will be measured out and rebuilt also, and prosperity is going to return.' "

In a second vision, Zechariah saw four horns. When he asked the angel-interpreter what they were, he got the answer: "These are the horns (symbols of power) which scattered Israel and Judah." Perhaps they stood for four enemy nations.

A second look revealed four smiths. The angel said that these were sent by God to overcome the four horns that had beaten Judah down.

Chapter 2 opens with another "measuring line" vision.

"Where are you going?" the prophet asked the man who held the line.

"I am off to measure Jerusalem."

"Better get going in a hurry," a couple of angels said to the man, "and while you are at it tell the boss of the project that Jerusalem is not to have any walls this time. There will be so many people and so much livestock here that it will be like open country. Anyway, the Lord says that the divine glory will be all the wall of protection the new city will ever need.

"So, call in the survivors of the people God spread to the four winds. Tell them to return from Babylon and the nations who plundered them. They are still the apple of the Lord's eye, and now God is going to shake up their conquerors until the tables are turned and the former masters are serving them. Tell them to come back to Zion and God will live there in their midst, and all the nations will finally come there to worship the Lord of Israel.

"It is time now for every living thing to be silent and wait before the Lord Who is about to move into action again."

Along with Zerubbabel, the governor, a priest named Joshua shared the leadership of the returned Jews in Judah. Zechariah told the people that he, Zechariah, had seen a vision of how the Lord had checked Joshua out thoroughly and put the heavenly "O.K." on him (chapter 3).

"I saw Joshua the high priest standing before an angel of the Lord, with the heavenly lawyer for the prosecution, Satan, standing beside him." Evidently Satan had been fulfilling his role as specially-appointed "adversary" (the "devil" role that Satan has in later writings like the New Testament has not been attached to him yet in Jewish thought). We don't hear the "case" against Joshua; we just hear God's judgment in Zechariah's vision. "You lose this one, Satan," the Lord said. "Jerusalem is like a brand I have plucked from the burning fire at the last moment." And turning to Joshua the Lord said to the angel, "Take those dirty clothes off him. Dress him up in clean clothes and a new turban."

After Joshua was cleaned up, the angel told him why the Lord had ordered that to be done. "As long as you keep the Lord's commandments carefully, you will be in charge of the temple, and you will have an open line of communication with us here in heaven. The 'Branch' will work with you (Zerubbabel?), and the precious stone you will wear as high priest will be a sign that through your intercession the guilt of this land is taken away each day. There will be prosperity and peace for all the people."

This same angel kept coming back to visit with the prophet. Chapter 4 tells about the time he woke up Zechariah and said "What do you see?" What Zechariah saw was a gold lampstand with a bowl on top of it, and then seven more lamps on top of the bowl, each with something like an eyelid. These lamps are not lights you look at; these are lamps like eyes that look at you. A little later the angel tells him that these are, indeed, the seven eyes of the Lord that see everything that goes on in the whole world. On each side of the big lampstand is an olive tree.

Zechariah was a little confused. He hated to have to ask, but he did, "What is all this?"

The angel seemed surprised that he didn't know. "Don't you know what these things represent?"

"No, actually I confess that I don't," the prophet had to admit.

"This is the word of the Lord to Zerubabbel: 'Not by might, not by power, but by My Spirit,' says the Lord of Hosts. 'Continue to lean on Me and the great mountain of difficulties and obstacles will be smoothed out, and he will see the capstone of the temple placed with shouts of praise.' " Then to make sure Zechariah caught all the meaning of the more poetic language, the angel repeated the message. "What I am saying is that Zerubbabel started building the temple and he is going to get to finish it. All the people who saw only the little day by day work and difficulties when this project got underway will see him put the top stone in place."

"Thanks," the prophet murmured, "but could you make the meaning of the two olive trees which stand on each side of the lampstand of God just as plain to me?"

"Just think about that a minute," the angel prodded. "Who are the two persons God has anointed to stand by to see that God's commandments are carried out? The head of the church and the head of the state. High priest and governor, or king, right?"

Start to read chapter 5 and you almost duck instinctively. Who wants to be hit with a flying scroll thirty feet long and fifteen feet wide?

"Now, what is that?" Zechariah asked his angel friend.

"That," the angel replied, "is the curse that goes over the whole country. It flies over the land and settles on everyone who steals or bears false witness about someone else. Those sins bring ruin to the person and his/her house.

"And while we are thinking about wickedness," the angel continued, "look at this."

"What is it?" Zechariah had to ask again.

"It's a big jar with this lead top on it. It's going around the land like the flying scroll." A quick look inside revealed a woman sitting down in it. She tried to get out, but the angel slapped the lid back on the jar. "We have to keep her inside," the angel explained. "She represents wickedness that fills the land."

Just then, two other women flew in, with big wings like those of a stork. These were "the good gals (guys?)," so maybe there are twice as many good women as bad. They picked up the jar of wickedness and flew off with it.

"Where are they going with that jar?"

"To Babylon (Shinar)," the angel answered. "They are going to leave it there. It will be a good home for wickedness."

No sooner had the flying women and the jar disappeared than Zechariah saw four chariots coming out from between two bronze mountains. Red horses pulled the first one; black horses the second; white horses the third; and dappled horses the fourth.

"I suppose you want to know what these are?" the angel asked.

"I do," Zechariah admitted.

"They go out in all four directions to see that the Lord's

Spirit is being obeyed everywhere. Especially the Lord is concerned about the north country (Babylon)." And since the horses were champing at the bit to go, the angel told them to be off on their mission.

While the black horses and chariot go toward Babylon, an idea came from the Lord to Zechariah about how to use three important Jews who had just come in from Babylon. They were to go with the prophet to the house of Joshua, the high priest, with a silver and gold crown they had made. It's not quite clear whether the crown goes finally on Zerubbabel's head or Joshua's, but Joshua is to be assured that Zerubbabel will finish the temple project, and that he will rule in peace while the high priest stands by his side. The crown will stay in the temple as a constant reminder of how the church and the state are to work peaceably side by side. These new arrivals from Babylon can assure Josiah and all the original workers that help is on the way from the outside if they will only obey God and keep building.

Two years after the temple building began, a delegation from Bethel (the center of opposition by the Samaritans to the Jewish resurgence) paid Zechariah a call. They claimed they had a serious concern. "We have been observing two days each year as days of fasting and mourning for what happened to old Jerusalem and the temple about seventy years ago. Should we keep that up, or is this new building going to mean we can quit doing that each year?"

"The Lord says 'I am not so sure that your fast days were any more motivated by your concern for Me than your feast days which you enjoy so much! Back in the days when the land around here was prosperous, before the Babylonian conquest, the true prophets gave the people My word that what I wanted was fair judgment, kindness and mercy in all H.B. dealings with each other. They spelled it out: no oppression of orphans or widows, foreigners or poor people, and nobody even wanting in his/her heart to take advantage of someone else. That was the kind of 'religious ' practice I wanted to see. But they turned a deaf ear and a cold shoulder to the true prophets; they made sure they never listened to the Spirit message. I called and called, but they wouldn't hear, so I scattered them among the nations and left this homeland desolate.'

"But there is more," Zechariah continued (chapter 8). "The Lord is still determined to look after Mt. Zion, and when this temple is built God will return to live here. Once again this will be the holy mountain in the holy city. The surviving people from other countries will come back here to live in righteousness and faithfulness, not as their parents did. Jerusalem will be a safe place for little children and for the oldest people.

"All this is happening because the temple is being rebuilt. So we aren't going to stop now. Before this project started there was no prosperity here for people or for animals, and nobody was safe here from the enemies who didn't want to see this rebuilding of Jerusalem succeed. But now the Lord is giving rain and prosperity along with peace. There is going to be as much blessing for this remnant now as there was trouble before.

"Trust God and keep working! This time don't forget to practice real religion that makes any society blessed. Tell the truth in your dealings with each other, and in every case where judgment is passed. Let all court decisions be perfectly fair. Never swear falsely, and never consider doing anything that would hurt a brother or sister citizen."

"Good speech, I'm sure," one of the visitors from

Bethel may have replied, "but what about the fast days in the fifth and seventh months, not to mention the fourth and tenth-month fast days?"

"Don't you see how it all ties in?" Zechariah finished up. "With all these promises from the Lord, there can't be anything but rejoicing, so those old days of mourning are going to be days of joy and feasting. Right here in Jerusalem is going to be where it all happens. People will be coming from everywhere in the world to seek the Lord's favor here. Every time a Jew starts a pilgrimage to Jerusalem from any other country, ten people or more will want to tag along saying 'We have heard that God is with you Jews.' "

The editor of the book didn't even bother to say how the jealous leaders of Samaria felt about that kind of talk. Since their opposition only intensified, we can surmise that they joined others who said "We've heard that kind of talk from the Jews before!"

Land of Beginning Again

"All the nations belong to the Lord anyway," the poems of chapter 9 go on to say. "Syria, as well as Israel, is the Lord's. And the coastal city-states of Tyre and Sidon, rich as they are, will be stripped of their wealth and ruined because they have not been obedient to the Lord. So will the cities of Philistia. One day they will be absorbed in Judah the way the Jebusites were when David took their city and made it into his capital called Jerusalem. There will be peace because the Lord will be the acknowledged ruler of all.

"What a time for rejoicing that will be. The king of Judah will come into Jerusalem riding on a donkey as kings come when they come in peace."(9:9) Five hundred years later the Jews were still much aware of Zechariah's promise when Jesus acted out this prophecy as He entered Jerusalem a week before His crucifixion. "Horses and chariots and instruments of war will not be needed any longer because this God-annointed king will reign over the whole world in peace.

"Before that happens the people of Judah and Israel will be restored to enough military strength to follow the Lord to victory over Greece whose forces will be trampled. God is caring especially for Judah as the Chosen People, making Judah's young men and women flourish like a full crop of grain or new wine from an abundant harvest."

"And yet," the poems continue in chapter 10, "people still persist in asking the fertility cult images to give them rain for their crops, or they go to fortunetellers to inquire about prospects of the weather. Don't they know the Lord brings the spring rains for the growing season? The Lord alone controls the storm clouds. No wonder the people wander like sheep without a shepherd. And no wonder God is going to punish the leaders who lead them astray.

"The Lord is not going to let Chosen Israel fall again. This is a multiple-choice test. Israel is to the Lord like: (check one)

_____ a prize horse for battle

_____ the cornerstone for building a new world

_____ the peg that holds the whole tent upright

_____ the Lord's battle bow for fighting

_____ the source of every annointed ruler

_____ ALL OF THE ABOVE.

"Check the last one, world, because the Lord will transform Israel from a band of sheep subject to foreign shepherds to a mighty battle unit which will trample all the foes of God. That's why the house of Judah and the people of Joseph are being brought back as though God had never rejected them. Yes, even the remnant of the old northern kingdom will be returned. Think of that and praise the Lord!

"God will whistle and they will come from all the far countries where they have been scattered, from Egypt, Assyria, back to this land. They will become so numerous that they will spread out again to Gilead and Lebanon as in the time of David's kingdom. More than that, they will go back across the Red Sea and up the Nile into the heart of Egypt again, this time as conquerors. Proud

Assyria will now bow before them as well, until the glory of the Lord is acknowledged by all.

"Too bad, false shepherds! You've lost your sheep. Too bad, lions who ravaged My people! All the great forests and woods are gone, and there is no place for you even to hide." (If you ever meet Zechariah, ask him if that is what the Lord is saying in the opening verses of chapter 11.)

Meanwhile, if the shepherds of the flock of Israel are going to sell their own sheep for slaughter (with the nerve then to thank the God of Israel for making them rich at the expense of the flock), then the prophet will have to become the shepherd acting for the Lord. So Zechariah pictures himself as the shepherd, a shepherd who has two staffs (or a rod and a staff). One staff is named "Grace," since it is only by God's grace that the flock is allowed to continue. The other is named "Union," because the two former kingdoms of Israel should be united.

Actually, God is the shepherd, the prophet only the spokesman here. Verse 8 says that God destroyed three shepherds, though nobody knows just which rulers or leaders are indicated. Anyway, God is pictured as giving up on the flock again.

"I won't be your shepherd anymore," the Lord-shepherd says. "You can just go ahead and destroy yourselves."

To act that out, the shepherd takes the staff called "Grace" and breaks it. "This breaks the covenant God made with this people. I am quitting this job and going home." Then Zechariah continued his little show by telling the listeners: "I told the people in charge, 'If you are so inclined, you might pay me my wages as of this date.' They did. I can't believe how generous they were. They weighed out thirty shekels of silver, which is the price of an injured slave! I took the silver and put it into the offering plate in the temple—because it really showed how much or how little they thought the Lord's care was worth to them."

So saying, he took the second staff and broke it before them.

"The "union" between Judah and Israel is broken forever as well," he said.

"From now on," the Lord told Zechariah, "this land will have a shepherd who doesn't care one bit for the sheep. This shepherd doesn't look for the lost or strayed ones, never tends the wounds of hurt sheep, and doesn't even provide food for the sound ones. He is more like an animal devouring the flock instead of protecting it! But woe to that worthless shepherd who deserts the flock! May he lose the use of his arm and the sight of his eye."

We wonder how many "leaders" of the nation took those remarks personally.

Being a prophet in Old Testament days wasn't easy. Neither is trying to interpret what he meant 2500 years later. However, we get the central point of the last three chapters of the book, even though we probably miss a good many details. Chapter 12 opens with the Lord saying that Jerusalem is going to win out against all its enemies in the countryside of Judah and in all the world. The other nations will find that picking on Jerusalem is going to be like picking up a stone only to realize that it is so heavy that it strains the lifter. Even if all the nations ally themselves in war against Jerusalem, the Lord will strike the horses and riders with blindness and insanity. Then the rest of the people in Judah will be able to see that Jerusalem is defended by the Lord God.

"Once the rest of Judah sees the light, all of Judah

together will be like a flaming torch in a shock of dry grain. That fire will burn up everything around them, but Jerusalem will not be touched. And the Lord will probably arrange it so that the initial victories will belong to the clans of Judah outside Jerusalem, just so Jerusalem won't be too puffed up with pride. Then the house of David will be the strongest ruling house in the world. Even the weakest soldier of Jerusalem will be as strong as the angel of the Lord who leads them in battle, because God's own spirit will fill them."

Strangely enough, 12:10 changes the mood entirely. Instead of wild rejoicing as an invincible conqueror, Jerusalem is suddenly filled with bitter grief. For some reason, the people of the city are pictured as having killed a favorite son. Perhaps this is a personification of their coming to realize how many people have been hurt in their unjust society. Now they begin to cry, wailing even louder than the worshippers of the dead god, Hadadrimmon. But this crying is not a public show; this is a private grief that men and women feel in private, not even with their families. The crying, the genuine repentance for their sins, becomes a fountain that cleanses them of guilt so they can be free to serve the Lord in faithfulness. (The reader is left to decide, perhaps, whether there is not more real strength and victory in genuine confession than in the first picture of fiery annihilation of other people.)

"On that day," says the Lord, "I will remove all the idols that tempt My people to worship other gods. Also, because the temple and the Law are here, I will not allow any more prophets or preachers to claim that he or she is speaking for Me. If one tries to prophesy in My name, his own parents will kill him or her if necessary to stop such blasphemy. No more men wearing hairy mantles will be honored, not even to themselves. Instead, if anyone asks 'Are you a prophet?' the answer will come, 'Heavens, no. I am just a farmer working my own family's land.' Then if anyone asks, 'What are these wounds on your back? They look like the kind of marks of mutilation that those crazy prophets make on themselves when they are in a frenzy!' The answer will be, 'Oh, those? I got those from my friends when we had a little drinking bout one night at their house.' ''

Prophecy must have hit a low point because of so much false and misleading preaching. Or maybe it is always true that misleading propaganda in the name of the Lord is in the same category as idolatry. Both lead people away from centering their attention on the will of the One true God.

Now, in 13:7-9, we run into another "shepherd" passage like those of chapter 11. This time the human shepherd, a high priest or governor, has been faithful, but the flock hasn't. When the leader is struck down it is because of the wickedness of the people. Only a third of them will be left when the Lord is through with them, and they will have to be refined like gold in the fire of testing. This remnant will then be God's real people because they will call on God only for help.

By the time *Zechariah* is written, the Jews had developed a kind of literature which scholars call "apocalyptic" (like *Ezekiel* 38-39). It deals with some prophetic disclosure of things to come, usually dealing with the end of the present age of world history. The last chapter of *Zechariah* is an example.

"The day of the Lord is coming! The final battle between Israel and its enemies will begin. At first the combined forces of all the nations will overrun Jerusalem, plundering everything. Rape and pillage will be the order of the day, and half the people of the city will be killed or taken captive. The half of the populace who are left have absolutely no hope until, suddenly, the Lord appears like a super-giant warrior. He stands on the Mount of Olives, just east of the city, and the mountain splits in two. Just as in the days of Uzziah, king of Judah, when the terrible earthquake occurred in the Jerusalem area, people will flee in panic while the new-rift valley forms running east and west through the mount.

"Now the Lord is on the scene, with an angelic host. The weather is neither cold nor hot; and there is no darkness even at night. Great springs of fresh water will burst out of Jerusalem, with half of the supply flowing east toward the desert as *Ezekiel* 47:1-12 envisioned, but half moving out toward the sea on the west. The flow will be constant summer and winter. And there will be no ruler of the earth except the Lord God.

"All the land of ancient Judah will be leveled except the site of Jerusalem. The city will remain on a pinnacle where its inhabitants will always be secure from attack. Meanwhile, the Lord's main weapon against the enemies that almost overcame Judah will be plague. It will come so quickly that people's flesh will rot while they are still standing, with eyes and tongues rotting away. Such panic will seize the invaders that they will begin to fight among themselves. Even Judah's people will fight the people of Jerusalem. Before it is over, the wealth of all the surrounding nations will be collected, while their armies lose even their livestock to the plague of rot.

"Naturally, this will teach the survivors of the other nations a good lesson. They will come ever after to Jerusalem's temple to celebrate the feast of booths when the Lord is declared king. Since anyone who doesn't come misses the part of the celebration where the gift of water is honored, they will not get any rain from the Lord for their crops. In Egypt, where they don't depend on rain for the Nile's water, the Lord will send plague to those who don't come to Jerusalem.

"Divine rule will be so complete that even the bells on the horses' harness will bear the inscription "Holy to the Lord." All common work will be sacred. There will be no need for 'sacred' vessels in the temple, because every cookpot and serving bowl in every home will be just as holy. And no longer will anyone have to stay in the temple to make sure that unclean things are traded for 'clean.' Everything will be clean; every bit of life in that great 'Day' will be sacred."

That always seems to be the bottom line to the visions of all the great prophets: everything is God's as, indeed, it always was.

MALACHI

Ring Out the Old

The little Jewish community around Jerusalem, to which Haggai and Zechariah spoke their pieces, had completed the new temple and had settled down to business as usual. A governor appointed by Persia controlled the political life; Ezra and Nehemiah hadn't shown up yet to stir up a religious reform that would tackle the problem of Jewish men marrying "foreign" women. So this little book, the last of the Old Testament, leaves us about 450 years before the birth of Jesus and the beginning of New Testament times.

We don't know the prophet's name. He simply goes by "Malachi" which means "Messenger," and he brought a message from the Lord which not many people wanted to hear. Some people don't think that his opening portrayal of God as a father is very appealing. This father, according to the first five verses, not only shows favoritism in that He loves one son better than another, He actually goes out of His way to destroy Esau because He hates that son so much. And He tells Jacob, the favored son, that no matter how much Esau may rebuild He will keep tearing up everything he makes. His anger toward Esau is forever, He assures Jacob.

Of course, this wasn't bad news for Jacob, or the people of Judah. They hated Esau, or Edom, so much that

this "message" from the Lord was just what they liked
to hear. What they didn't want to hear was what follows
from verse 6 on.

"If I am the Parent Who loves you so much, am I not
supposed to be getting a little honor, if not fear, around
here? You want to know how you have dishonored Me?
I'll lay it out for you:

"You have been offering polluted food on My altar.
Instead of the 'best' of the flock, I've been getting blind,
lame, and sick animals. Try passing off stuff like that on
the governor and see how much he appreciates it. Is that
the way you ought to approach Me when you come asking favors? No, I'm not going to take that from you. In
all the other nations where I am worshipped, the incense
is pure and the gifts they offer are the best, but your
priests apparently don't think that I rate high enough to
be treated reverently. And I have special contempt for
anyone who vows to sacrifice the best of the flock and
then substitutes a blemished animal. No great king would
stand for that, and I, the Lord of all the nations, won't
either!

"So listen closely, you priests, if you don't begin right
now to do your job of giving glory to Me, you will pay
for it. In fact, I am already putting a curse on everything
you do. Notice how the offerings have dropped? You'll
be lucky to get anything more than the entrails (dung)
of the animals you sacrifice.

"I made a covenant with Levi, promising life and peace
for him and his descendants if they served well as My
priests. He was honest and taught the truth, a good
example who turned many people from their sin. That
still is the model which priests should follow. But you
turn people away from My way. Your 'teaching' actually
leads them to do wrong. The 'judgments' you make in

the people's court are not true to My Law but are your own decisions. You have corrupted the covenant of Levi, and you are going to be shamed before all the people because you have."

(Scholars who date this writing around 450 B.C., before the time of Ezra, point out that the Jews are still going with the Deuteronomic Code which was adopted under Huldah's urging in 622 B.C. It allowed Levites to be priests, (see *Deuteronomy* 18:1-8) though no "covenant with Levi" is mentioned anywhere else in the Old Testament except here in *Malachi*. After Ezra, the Priestly Code limited priesthood to descendants of Aaron only; Levites were assigned custodial and police jobs around the temple area. Any sections of the Old Testament we have read which emphasized the priesthood of Aaron were written or edited after Ezra's day. Perhaps this shoddy, nonprofessional work of the Levitical priests which *Malachi* condemns prompted Ezra and others to kick them out of the priests' union a few years later.)

"When there is no proper reverence for God, then social injustice grows because human life loses its sacredness too." Malachi is sure of that.

Malachi is also concerned about the problem of intermarriage of Jewish male leaders with foreign women, the problem with which Ezra and Nehemiah dealt so harshly a few years later. Verse 10 of chapter 2 seems to be a statement that all people of all nations are created equal as children of God. A closer look reveals that Malachi is talking only of the Hebrew family, and he goes on to say that it is an affront to God when Hebrew men marry outside the family. When a Jewish man divorces his own Jewish wife in order to marry the daughter of a foreign god, things have gone too far. One who does this should be barred from church and cut off from the community!

"You can come to the altars of God and weep barrels of tears, but God isn't going to accept any offering from one who is faithless to the wife of his younger days. Marriage is a covenant between the two, and between them and God. God wants them to have children raised in the proper Hebrew tradition. Divorce is really breaking a covenant with God. Along with violence and injustice, God hates divorce," Malachi says.

"While we are at it, let me say that God is getting tired also of those who say that God doesn't seem to care whether a person does good or evil. They think that if they raise a theological question about the justice of God they can be excused for whatever they do or don't do.

"A special messenger from the Lord is going to have to come and clean up things so the Lord can live in full glory in the temple (chapter 3). But when the messenger comes, who can stand the thorough cleaning and refining job that must be done? The priests of Levi's household will be purified so that they can perform their priestly functions the way they used to, and God will be pleased again to accept their offerings. Then God's judgment will be swift. People who hurt other people by misleading them with sorceries, or breaking up marriages, or bearing false witness, or by taking unfair advantage of working people, widows, orphans, or strangers, and who do not show proper reverence for God, will have to face that judgment.

"We are dealing now with the same God all the old prophets spoke about. Through them the Lord begged our ancestors to return to living by the Law, so that the Lord could return to them. We still haven't come back.

" 'How do we do that?' you ask. One simple answer is: stop trying to rob God! When you don't bring your full tithes to the storehouse of the temple, that is what you are doing. You expect to pay your bills for food, clothing and shelter, don't you?" Well, God is the original producer! You expect tenants to pay the landlord full rent, don't you? The earth is the Lord's and we have to pay up.

"Go ahead and test the Lord. Bring the full tithes, so there wil be provisions for the temple staff and food to share with the needy, and see if God won't bless you with even more produce. You will be a model for all the nations." Evidently all the nation did not rush to accept Malachi's challenge to tithe because Nehemiah had to adopt strict methods later to collect them.

" 'What's the use? you say. People who don't serve God get along just as well as those who do. Often they seem to be rewarded all the more. They rob God and get away with it.'

"That isn't correct. People who try to keep God's will are recorded in a book, and none of them will be forgotten on that Day when the Lord acts to judge the world. And these will be spared when God makes it plain as to the ones who have served and the ones who have not.

"For, behold (chapter 4), the Day is coming when all the arrogant wrongdoers will be burned up like dry stubble in a field. But for those who reverence God, the sun will rise with new life. Like young animals in the fresh morning, they will share the joy that Life brings. Then there will be no doubt about the wicked getting their just reward. Also the good!"

P.S., an editor adds, since this is the last manuscript in the whole collection of prophets, "Remember to keep all the commandments of the Law."

P.P.S., another tacked on, "In case you think that Malachi expects a priest to be God's 'messenger' who cleans up the temple worship and introduces the Day of the Lord (which he probably did), the 'messenger' is going to be none other than Elijah coming back to us. He will get family life and national life restored and will prepare the way for the Lord."

On that note, the Old Testament ends. And on that note the New Testament begins. "It all fits right in," they said when they wondered where their new stories of Jesus belonged. "Obviously John, the baptist, is Elijah, and the Lord for Whom he prepares the way is Jesus, the Messiah."